MYSTERIES AND LEGENDS SERIES

MYSTERIES AND LEGENDS

OF GEORGIA

TRUE STORIES
OF THE UNSOLVED AND UNEXPLAINED

DON RHODES

Guilford, Connecticut

To Ralph McGill, Minnie Pearl, Michael Guido, Chuck Sprowls, Shirley Chisholm, James Brown, Ella Sampert Rhodes, Reginald Wells, Don Carter, Ada Wren Collins, Leonard and Ruben Rhodes, Ethel Maddox Smith, Ike and Justine Washington, Harold Sprowls, Bill Lowery, Jerry Clower, Kaye Mann, Casey Jenkins, Erskine Caldwell, Paul Hemphill, Irving Waugh, Inez Wylds, Roy "Pop" Lewis, Marie Sampert Ballard, Irby Mandrell, Carolyn Usry, Teddy Wilburn, John Thomason, Johnnie Bailes, Lloyd Lindroth, O. B. McClinton, Will Fahnoe, Joe Usry, Lester Maddox, John Barnes, Ogden Doremus, Lester Flatt, and other late legends who have let me into their personal worlds and enriched my life.

To buy books in quantity for corporate use
or incentives, call **(800) 962-0973**
or e-mail **premiums@GlobePequot.com**.

Text design: Lisa Reneson, Two Sisters Design
Layout: Sue Murray
Map: M. A. Dubé © Morris Book Publishing, LLC

Library of Congress Cataloging-in-Publication Data

Rhodes, Don.
  Mysteries and legends of Georgia : true stories of the unsolved and unexplained / Don Rhodes.
    p. cm.
  Includes bibliographical references.
  ISBN 978-0-7627-5425-0
  1. Georgia—History—Anecdotes. 2. Georgia—History, Local—Anecdotes. 3. Georgia—Biography—Anecdotes. 4. Curiosities and wonders—Georgia. 5. Legends—Georgia. I. Title.

  F286.6.R48 2010
  398.209758—dc22

2009034918

Printed in the United States of America
10 9 8 7 6 5 4 3 2 1

CONTENTS

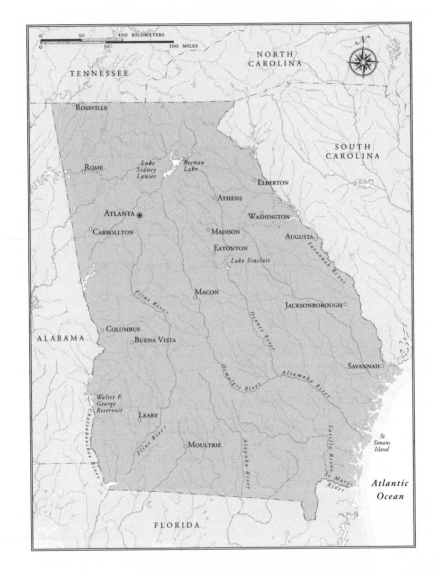

GEORGIA

ACKNOWLEDGMENTS

First of all, thanks to my life partner and closest friend, Ervin Edward "Eddie" Smith Jr., for loving the more unique side of life and being curious to want to know more about it. He is living proof that you don't need a college degree to be smart about life in general.

And thanks to the great four-legged friends and confidants I've had in my life: Fluffy, Little Bit, Wolfie, Foxie, Reba, Jasper, Rusty, Willard, and Jayme Brown, who lifted me up when two-legged folks brought me down.

And, in no particular order, my gratefulness also goes out to my father, Ollen Columbus Rhodes, and his wife, Jean Swann Rhodes; my three sisters: Linda Groover and her husband, Sammy; Ann Holland and her husband, George; and Jan Jarriel and her husband, Jerry; my brothers: Larry Rhodes and his wife, Teresa; Mike Spence and his wife, Kathy; and Doug Spence and his wife, Bobbi, for always being supportive and loving; as well as my late mother, Ella Sampert Rhodes, who gave me my love of reading and music.

Special thanks this past year to my friends Duncan Wheale, Pat Claiborne, Jeff Barnes, Todd Beasley, Johnny Edwards, Kelley New, Lamar Garrard, Milledge Murray, Flo Carter, Jim

Taylor, Dan White, Free Pennington, Turner Simkins, Lou Brissie, Beverly Barnhardt, Lee (Sheridan) Lynn, David Hobbs, and Bill and Linda Macky for listening to my stories about researching this book and acting as though they really were interested.

And in these very tough times of transitions, special thanks at Morris Communications and *The Augusta Chronicle* to Kay Pruitt, Billy and Will Morris, Martha Jean McHaney, Elizabeth Adams, Tharon Giddens, Bill Kirby, Don Bailey, Mark Albertin, Sherry Fulmer, and Pete May for making me feel still useful and productive.

Also at the *Chronicle,* special thanks always to Sean Moores and Rhonda Hollimon for their generous assistance.

Thanks to Steve Bisson of the *Savannah Morning News*, Cara Pastore of the Georgia Department of Economic Development, Nancy Peeples of the Elberton Granite Association, John Rogers of the Pasaquan Preservation Society Inc. for help with photos; Stancel "Stan" May and Jan Page for their love of circus history; former U.S. Representative D. Douglas "Doug" Barnard Jr. and Atlanta-area resident Mike Ault for their insight into the Georgia Guidestones; Keith Shafer for educating me about the graves in St. Paul's Episcopal churchyard in Augusta; Tom Atkinson, Robert Thompson Atkinson Sr., Margaret Nix Ponder, and Paullin Judin for their memories of their amazing relative Lula Hurst Atkinson; Lewis Regenstein for his knowledge of the supposed lost Confederate gold; Sandra Scott Whitworth for telling me more about her parents' amazing Asian-theme house; *Three Faces of Eve* authors Hervey M. Cleckley and Corbett H. Thigpen for long ago telling me the background behind their book; Christine Costner Sizemore (Eve herself) for allowing me to become her friend; and Georgia Historical Society senior historian Stan Deaton for his expert views on Button Gwinnett's grave.

Of course, many thanks to the great friends I've made at Globe Pequot Press/Lyons Press in Guilford, Connecticut, and Helena, Montana, including Kathryn Mennone, Amy Alexander, Christine Etlinger, Shelley Wolf, and especially Erin Turner. It was Erin who suggested me for the *Mysteries and Legends of Georgia* project and who made my dreams come true with our successful joint collaborations in 2008: *Ty Cobb: Safe at Home* and *Say It Loud: My Memories of James Brown, Soul Brother No. 1.*

Extra-special thanks goes to the staff at Globe Pequot Press, including Bob Sembiante for being such a great publicist; former editor Allen Jones for offering me the contract for this new project; my wonderful editor, Meredith Davis Rufino, layout artist Sue Murray, text designer Lisa Reneson, and map graphic artist M. A. Dubé for guiding me to another book completion.

Finally, thanks to God for all the wonderful blessings that come from all the great friends and family members who continue to enrich my life. I'm so blessed.

PREFACE

Although I was born in Gainesville, Texas, I've lived in Georgia for most of my life. The huge Peach State always has intrigued me with its diversity of geography, ranging from its mighty mountains and the Atlantic seacoast to its flat rural farmland and old communities settled along the state's many broad rivers.

This same diversity has generated—and continues to generate—many mysteries and legends, usually resulting from the exploits of unique people or astounding events. Globe Pequot Press has offered me this chance to recount and explore many of them through its popular Mysteries and Legends series.

What I love about almost any writing project—whether books or articles—is that I usually learn as much new information as I hope that my readers will learn. However, when I started this particular project, I thought that there would be fewer new things to learn because of my familiarity with the state's history and famous figures. But, wow, was I wrong.

In beginning this project, I decided not to go after the weirder stories, such as reports of flocks of birds falling from the air like hailstones or people bursting into flames for no apparent reason or reports of UFO abductions. But I couldn't resist including the story of then-future U.S. president Jimmy Carter filing an official UFO-sighting report in his own handwriting (which certainly proved to be interesting reading).

And what I found through respected sources about the supposedly "lost gold" of the Confederacy really surprised me. After all, I wanted to believe that all that gold and silver really was somewhere around Washington, Georgia, just waiting to be found.

I had never heard of Lula Hurst, probably America's first "wonder woman," before starting this project, or of the fascinating, self-taught artist Eddie Owens Martin, who created his own world, which he called Pasaquan. He changed his name to St. EOM and believed that his upswept hairstyle was an antenna to his spiritual world. Honest.

I knew about George Washington's favorite nephew being buried in an Augusta churchyard and about the Waving Girl in Savannah. But I didn't know that when the widow of that favorite nephew remarried, her nuptials became the first wedding in the White House. And I didn't know that the Waving Girl greeted incoming and outgoing ships both day and night for more than forty years.

And who would have guessed that the chief of the Cherokee nation, who led more than fifteen thousand displaced Native Americans on the Trail of Tears from Georgia to Oklahoma, was none other than a Scottish American whose father was born in Scotland and whose mother was part Cherokee?

Growing up, I knew that Oscar-winning actress Susan Hayward lived in north Georgia, but I was interested to learn of her valiant attempts to live as an average, unknown Georgia citizen. Of course, that was virtually impossible.

Perhaps my favorite mystery was exploring the reason for a life-size statue of a baby elephant being in a Moultrie cemetery. In doing so, I discovered that a horrendous circus train accident happened right after the turn of the twentieth century around Columbus.

A number of mysteries most likely will never be solved, such as who built the giant Rock Eagle near Eatonton and the Georgia Guidestones (a smaller version of Stonehenge) near Elberton, or where Declaration of Independence signer Button Gwinnett is buried.

But the fun of those mysteries is that they stay unsolved for future generations to ponder and explore.

You can find many excellent books that lead you to other mysteries and legends in Georgia as well as other states. I hope you enjoy this one, though, and that it educates and entertains you as much as it did me.

CHAPTER 1

ELBERTON'S STONEHENGE AND DUTCHY

Northeast Georgia is full of many great mysteries. Two of them are connected to the town of Elberton, one of the nation's largest producers of granite memorial and building stones. Those two mysteries provoke the questions: Why was the Confederate statue of Dutchy buried in disgrace for eighty-two years? And what is behind the construction of the Georgia Guidestones, also described as America's Stonehenge?

Today you can find the seven-foot-tall statue of Dutchy in the Elberton Granite Museum and Exhibit, which was financed primarily by the Elberton Granite Association Inc. and its member organizations. The multipurpose building has 4,800 square feet of exhibit space on three levels and reflects Elberton's position as the nation's largest granite-quarrying and monument-manufacturing district. Among the exhibits in the museum is the Peter Bertoni Sea Lion, part lion and part fish, a good-luck symbol made in 1901 at Elberton's first granite plant. But the most popular exhibit is the statue of Dutchy.

The Civil War had been over for thirty-three years when the statue was unveiled on the town square on July 15, 1898. The Italian sculptor, Arthur Beter, apparently did not do his homework to fully understand how real Confederate soldiers and uniforms looked. The statue, which seemed to be wearing Northern clothes and appeared European, shocked and angered local residents, including many former Confederate soldiers. Almost immediately, local residents began to disdainfully call the statue "Dutchy" because they thought that, with its heavy mustache, it resembled a Pennsylvania Dutchman. Instead of being proud of the monument, which was intended to honor the sacrifices of Confederate soldiers, the residents were ashamed of it.

Their anger came to a boil on the morning of August 14, 1900, when a "lynch mob" threw ropes around the statue's neck and pulled it down from its pedestal. The fall broke the statue's legs from its torso and base. Dutchy was buried next to the pedestal five feet underground. And there Dutchy remained for nearly eighty-two years.

Shortly after the statue's burial, the *Elberton Star* newspaper reported: "Poor Dutchy! No longer will he frighten animals and cause them to run away, and no longer will the public have a chance to make fun of his manly bearing. His body lay in state Wednesday morning just where he fell, and where throngs of people went to view his highness for the last time, when he was buried at the foot of the monument."

The shed where Dutchy had been carved was purchased by Peter Bertoni, a stone carver who created Elberton's first monument plant. Many more American soldiers would die in World War I, World War II, the Korean War, and the Vietnam Conflict before Dutchy would again see the light of day. Eventually, the thought of Dutchy being buried began to bother some local residents and business leaders, who decided in late April 1982 that it was time to resurrect the statue. After all, the statue was believed to be the first carving of a human ever created from Elberton's granite. The Elberton Granite Association agreed to pay for all costs connected with the digging and replacement of concrete that had to be broken up for the statue's removal. Finally, in a pouring rain, crews located the statue and lifted it with a large crane from its muddy grave. They then took the statue to a local car wash for a high-pressure cleaning before taking it to the Elberton Granite Museum and Exhibit, where Dutchy's broken body was reassembled.

William A. Kelly, executive vice president of the association, told reporters that the organization hoped the resurrection of Dutchy would "contribute to a great appreciation of our area's history." Noting that the Elberton granite industry in 1982 was generating approximately $46 million in revenue annually to the local economy, Kelly remarked, "Old Dutchy just might be proud of what he started here in Elberton."

And, indeed, Dutchy did start something. Many online Web sites and print publications tell Dutchy's unique story and draw attention to Elberton's status as the "granite capital of the world." Granite from the Elberton area has found its way into monuments and markers in all fifty states and many foreign countries. It is estimated that more than one-third of the tombstones in the United States have been made from granite quarried in the Elberton area.

Perhaps the strangest and most mysterious use of granite from the Elberton area can be seen seven miles north of the city on a hill that contains the mysterious Georgia Guidestones.

The strange story of the guidestones began when a stranger allegedly walked into the office of Joe Fendley Sr., president of Elberton Granite Finishing Company, in June 1979 with an elaborate request to create a massive monument that would call for world conservation and "herald the coming of an age of reason."

The fifty-something man identified himself as Robert C. Christian but also told Fendley that that wasn't his real name. Fendley thought he detected a midwestern accent. Christian said that he represented a group of American patriots who believed in God and country and who wanted to remain anonymous. He said that the Elberton area was selected because of its rural nature (possibly able to survive a nuclear holocaust), because Christian's great-grandmother was from Georgia, and because the area allegedly had some sort of divine importance to Native Americans.

There actually is a historic marker located a few miles north of the Georgia Guidestones and three miles south of Hartwell on US 29 that reads:

Center of the World

This was the Ah-Ye-Li A-Lo-Hee, Center of the World to the Cherokee Indians. To this assembly ground from which trails radiate in many directions, they came to hold their councils, to dance and worship which were to them related functions, and to barter their hides, furs and blankets for the trade goods of the white men from Augusta and other settlements. At one time there was a move to establish here the Hart County seat. This site was also a noted roost in the days when the now extinct passenger pigeons migrated here in the autumn in such numbers that "their weight broke the tree limbs."

In the following years, Fendley would say many times that he sent Christian to Wyatt C. Martin, president of Granite City Bank, who listened to Christian's story and his plans for the massive monument. Martin allegedly insisted that Christian reveal his true identity and his financial backers but promised Christian that the information would never be revealed publicly. Martin apparently was satisfied and later told Fendley that Christian had deposited a large amount of money in the Granite City Bank and that the project could proceed. Christian supposedly showed up only one more time in Elberton at Fendley's office. He was carrying a shoebox, which he opened to show Fendley the model of the monument his anonymous group wanted erected.

About ten months later, between two hundred and three hundred people gathered seven miles north of Elberton off GA 77 leading to Hartwell for the unveiling of the Georgia Guidestones on the northern edge of Mildred and Wayne Mullenix's Double-Seven Ranch. The agreement with the Mullenix family allowed grazing rights for their livestock for two more generations, but the family was prohibited from planting shrubbery above nose height within the five acres designated as the monument's ground.

At the unveiling ceremony, U.S. Representative D. Douglas Barnard Jr. of Augusta, representing Georgia's Tenth Congressional District, pulled off the sheet of black plastic covering the monument. Barnard told the gathering that the ten guides inscribed on the monument in various languages warned that the United States must preserve its resources because society and government are limited.

Reminiscent of the ancient Stonehenge monument near Wiltshire, England, the Georgia Guidestones consist of six stones that weigh a total of 237,746 pounds. Four are huge upright stones that are 6 feet 6 inches wide, 16 feet 4 inches tall, and 1 foot 7 inches thick. Each of the four weighs 42,437 pounds. Engraved on the four main stones are the ten guides in eight major languages: English, Russian, Mandarin Chinese, Arabic, classical Hebrew, Swahili, Hindi, and Spanish. The guides, according to the English version, are as follows:

MAINTAIN HUMANITY UNDER 500,000,000 IN PERPETUAL BALANCE WITH NATURE.

GUIDE REPRODUCTION WISELY—IMPROVING FITNESS AND DIVERSITY.

UNITE HUMANITY WITH A LIVING NEW LANGUAGE.

RULE PASSION–FAITH–TRADITION—AND ALL THINGS WITH TEMPERED REASON.

PROTECT PEOPLE AND NATIONS WITH FAIR LAWS AND JUST COURTS.

LET ALL NATIONS RULE INTERNALLY RESOLVING EXTERNAL DISPUTES IN A WORLD COURT.

AVOID PETTY LAWS AND USELESS OFFICIALS.

BALANCE PERSONAL RIGHTS WITH SOCIAL DUTIES.

PRIZE TRUTH–BEAUTY–LOVE SEEKING HARMONY WITH THE INFINITE.

BE NOT A CANCER ON THE EARTH—LEAVE ROOM FOR NATURE—LEAVE ROOM FOR NATURE.

The capstone weighs 24,832 pounds and has engraved on its sides in four "dead languages" (classical Greek, Sanskrit, Babylonian cuneiform, and Egyptian hieroglyphs) this message: "Let these be guidestones to an age of reason."

*The Georgia Guidestones, located in a rural part of the state,
lure many mystified visitors each year.*

In addition to the four main stones and the capstone, there is a 20,957-pound center stone. Other parts of the overall project include four base support stones that weigh 4,875 pounds each—and a center base support stone that weighs 2,707 pounds. As if all of this isn't awesome enough, a hole drilled in the monument aligns with the North Star, with two slots cut to align with the summer and winter solstices and a hole cut in the capstone to provide a sundial.

Over the years, thousands of visitors, including some vandals and religious zealots, have found their way to the Georgia

Guidestones and gazed up at the mysterious monument. They have also watched the video at the Elberton Granite Museum and Exhibit in which Joe Fendley and Wyatt Martin relate their encounters with the mysterious Robert C. Christian.

Interestingly, the many Web sites and publications devoted to the Georgia Guidestones don't mention anyone else from Fendley's stone company or Martin's bank who remembers seeing the mysterious Christian. One is left wondering: Out of the roughly two hundred granite companies in the Elberton area, why did Christian pick Fendley's Elberton Granite Finishing Company for the massive project?

However, from the very beginning, Wyatt Martin contended that he knew who Christian and his organization really were. When the guidestones were unveiled in March 1980, an article distributed by the United Press International wire service reported, "Martin said he knows the true identity of the mysterious Robert Christian but he says he will keep it a secret." The UPI reporter then quoted Martin as saying, "When I die the secret will die with me."

Nevertheless, others have their doubts.

An equally amazing account is told by Michael Ault, a senior technical management consultant with TUSC software consultants who lives in Alpharetta, Georgia. In his blog (http://mikerault.blogspot.com) Ault tells of his own visit to photograph and videotape the Georgia Guidestones:

> As I was wandering around the site video taping and taking pictures an older gentleman and his wife drove up,

he got out and his wife waited in the truck. Tall (about six-foot) and a little heavy although not overly so, he reminded me of several rural Georgia farmers I have met in my wanderings. He told me that he had heard someone had vandalized the stones and wanted to see how badly. We struck up a conversation and I asked him about the mystery surrounding who had them erected. He asked if I had heard the story and I said I read it on the Web.

He then stated: "All of that is bullshit." And smiled at me. He continued, "I worked at the [Pyramid] quarry when this was built. Mr. Fendley himself had it built and made up that story. He liked publicity, and Lord knows this gave it to him."

Ault said that the man, who identified himself as the foreman of Fendley's Pyramid Quarry at the time, confronted Fendley about the true origins of the monument. Ault quoted the foreman as saying, "He didn't deny it. He looked mad, but kind of half smiled at me."

Jim Miles's book *Weird Georgia: Close Encounters, Strange Creatures, and Unexplained Phenomena* states that the foreman at the Pyramid Quarry at that time was Joe Davis, and the book also identifies the person who actually engraved the guidestones as sandblaster Charlie Clamp.

I tracked down Ron Clamp, Charlie Clamp's son, who owns and operates Stonecrafters Farm near Elberton, which specializes in engraving monuments anywhere in the continental

United States. When I asked Clamp whether his father thought that Fendley, rather than Christian, was the actual originator of the guidestones, he replied by e-mail:

It took a while for me to reply because I wanted to speak to my father first, preferably on a day when his memory was sharp.

I was really young when he carved the guidestones, probably 17 or 18 years old. I helped with the stencil application, carried sand and helped clean up but that was the extent of any involvement I had.

I remember [Fendley quarry foreman] Mr. Davis, having met him and spent some time with him while the stones were being carved. I also met and became personally acquainted with Joe Fendley, and feel I knew him fairly well. When I first went into business for myself I moved into Fendley's old offices [apparently where the mysterious Christian first met Fendley and later showed up with the shoebox].

Joe Davis was a good quarrier, and Joe Fendley would have considered him a strong asset, but I can assure you that Fendley would have never confided anything of any importance to him about the guidestones. I can tell you numerous stories about how close an old file Fendley was.

If, first, someone did require him to keep secret who commissioned the stone or, second, if he just wanted to make the stones seem mysterious, then either way he would have kept it totally secret. My dad didn't know who was behind the project and didn't really care. There were magazines that said he heard strange voices while he was carving the stone. My dad is deaf enough from sandblasting that he was doing good to hear someone talking to him when it was quiet.

Another credible resource who has doubts that Christian and his organization really existed is none other than former U.S. Representative D. Douglas Barnard Jr., who actually pulled away the black plastic uncovering the guidestones on March 22, 1980.

When I contacted him at his Augusta home, Barnard told me:

Well, first of all I knew the stonecutter, Joe Fendley, very well, and the banker, Wyatt Martin, as well. Joe came to me one time and told me he was doing a Stonehenge kind of thing north of Elberton, and that he was doing it in conjunction with Wyatt Martin. He told me the mysterious story that Wyatt had been contacted by this fellow named Christian and had come up with this plan to do the stones.

Well, I was suspicious of this thing. Nothing actually was told me that I could put any confidence in, and I never did know who the third party really was. But, I believed Joe [about his sincerity in doing the project]. He was nothing but a stonecutter who had a granite company that cut stones. But as for the rest of the story, it was just hard for me to believe.

Thinking back two decades, Barnard recalled:

Fendley had come to Elberton from Alabama. He was an accountant and became an accountant for a stone company and then was able to buy the company. Now that's true. I knew Fendley and his wife and two children. He had a political appetite. He ran for mayor [of Elberton] three or four times and [was] elected at least two times. He had a vivid imagination. He thought one time he was going to be named the administrator of the [U.S.] Veterans Administration. He had known some people in Washington, and they indicated his name would be suggested to be head of the Veterans Administration.

In his last few years, Fendley was in the V.A. hospital here in Augusta. He pestered the life out of me and [Augusta lawyer] David Bell to get him out. So he finally got out and was being taken care of by his daughter and her husband. A minister took him in and housed him in a trailer and he later died. But, as close a friend as we were, he never admitted to me the details [of the guidestones].

I'll tell you one thing. I haven't been as inquisitive as you have been, but it always was a mystery to me, and

I always thought it was [created by] somebody who was absolutely crazy. . . . I do think Fendley and Martin were in cahoots. I don't think there was a fellow named Christian. And the way the granite business [was], it wouldn't have taken too much money to have done it.

You're on the right track as far as it being a mystery. It definitely is a mystery. The most powerful people in Elberton didn't know a thing about this.

Barnard said that on the day of the unveiling, it crossed his mind that maybe he was being drawn into some sort of a joke or hoax. "I felt very uncomfortable, frankly," Barnard said. "I thought maybe I was. I just didn't understand it. I can't remember what I said. I must have been ad-libbing really well that day, but it really was something else."

As for the alleged originator of the project, Robert C. Christian, apparently he was never heard from again. One can only assume that this mystery man and members of his secret patriotic organization must have slipped into the area secretly to see what was done with their money—unless, of course, neither Robert C. Christian nor his patriotic organization ever existed. But who really cares? For the guidestones remain one of the strangest, most interesting, and most mysterious attractions of the state of Georgia.

CHAPTER 2

THE REAL "EVE" AND HER THREE FACES

On May 7, 1953, two virtually unknown psychiatrists from Augusta, Georgia, shook up the world of mental health and ignited worldwide interest when they delivered their research paper based on the case of a woman patient who, they claimed, suffered from multiple personalities over which she had no control.

To protect her privacy and their doctor-patient relationship, Drs. Hervey M. Cleckley and Corbett H. Thigpen referred to the troubled housewife as "Eve." According to them, she would morph into the personalities of "good girl" Eve White, "party girl" Eve Black, and a stable personality known as Jane.

The wire services distributed news accounts of Cleckley and Thigpen's presentation to the American Psychiatric Association in Los Angeles, California, and the enormous public response led them to write about the case in their book *The Three Faces of Eve* (1957). It would sell millions of copies and be translated into many languages. The book was made into a movie in 1957.

In an Oscar-winning performance, Joanne Woodward portrayed Eve, the woman with three personalities.

"Not only did we give a report presenting our paper on the patient, but we also showed a film of the patient," Dr. Thigpen recalled twenty years later. "Dr. Cleckley and I were astonished at the interest our case generated. We thought it would be of interest only to people in the psychology field. When I came out of that meeting, I remember there were about fifteen to twenty reporters from all over the United States asking me questions. I didn't think it was unusual because reporters often covered the national convention in the past. But before we left Los Angeles, we received many calls and telegrams from all over the nation."

Dr. Cleckley said that the strangest letters came from people who felt that the multiple personalities of Eve were a result of witchcraft or spirit possessions. "I remember one person accused me of being spiritualistically illiterate," Cleckley said with a laugh. "This case is one that has aroused interest over a long period of time. It seems to be a thing that takes the fancy of many people including those who read magic things into it. We even thought once of writing a book of the more than one hundred letters we received of these ideas of possession, but we discarded the idea. I received one letter from Australia berating me for not realizing that it was reincarnation of three spirits getting in one body at the same time."

Years later the public would respond somewhat similarly to a woman called "Sybil," played by actress Sally Field in the 1976

COURTESY OF MIKE DEAS

Christine Costner Sizemore, the real Eve, has come to grips with her multiple personalities and the public's fascination with them.

movie of the same name, who supposedly suffered from sixteen distinct personalities. The tale of this young graduate student (in reality Shirley Ardell Mason) had a unique twist, with Sybil's psychiatrist being portrayed in the movie by none other than Joanne Woodward.

The mystery remaining for most fans of the book and movie versions of *The Three Faces of Eve* is: What ever happened to the real woman portrayed by Woodward? Did she ever become "normal" again? And, did she ever meet the actress who portrayed her on the big screen?

First, let's look at the real life of Eve, who revealed herself in 1975 by speaking publicly about mental health at Piedmont Technical College in Greenwood, South Carolina, and in 1977 by publishing *I'm Eve,* an autobiography.

Christine Costner was born on April 4, 1927, and grew up in Edgefield, South Carolina, not far from Augusta. She was the daughter of Eunice and Acie Costner.

"Both of my parents were big readers," she would later tell me. "I have a room in my house with nothing but books, including a collection that belonged to my parents. My mother loved [western novelist] Zane Grey and so did my dad. As a teenager, I read Shakespeare and other literature from high school. I think it is true of most of us who are readers that we identify with the subjects in the books we read."

As with most children, her life was filled with a lot of normal activities, such as listening to the Grand Ole Opry country music program broadcast live on Friday and Saturday nights from the WSM-AM radio station out of Nashville, Tennessee.

"Mother opened the living room window and set the radio in it, and our neighbors would line up and listen on the wraparound porch on the front side of the house," she told me in 2007. "In between the songs, our neighbors would argue about who was the best singer. It was a really neat time. At that time, I didn't think about it as socializing, but it really was."

She also loved hearing George Gershwin songs such as "I Got Rhythm" and admired Savannah, Georgia–born songwriter

Johnny Mercer's songs so much that she and her daughter Taffy would later visit his grave in Savannah's Bonaventure Cemetery. As she recalled: "He was a great entertainer."

One of her most vivid memories as a child was being held up to a coffin to touch the face of her dead grandmother. She lived near a sawmill and once saw a man mangled to death by the sawmill's blade. She also saw a drowned man stretched out on the ground. That would evoke the painful memories of being held up to touch her dead grandmother's hard, cold face and would cause Christine to run screaming through the woods. About this time, Christine began developing personalities who did things that Christine normally would not do. Nor could she explain why she did these things. She explained, "In school, they called me that lying girl. I always told them that it was not me that did the bad things, but the teacher even said I was lying because I didn't want to be punished."

She later would contend that she and Dr. Thigpen differed as to the origins of her multiple personalities. He thought the occurrences were things that "just happened," while Christine believed they were "self-imposed." As an example, she recalled:

When I was two years old, my mother cut her arm very badly and bled a great deal. She told me to run and get my father, but I ran away and hid under a pillow. Yet, I distinctly recall seeing a little girl get up and run and fetch my father. Perhaps what happened to me was the result of a guilt complex or because I was afraid of my mother. At any rate, it was about that time that my allergies started—one of my multiple personalities was allergic to animals, feathers and such throughout her existence.

Nobody really knows what traumas ignited Christine's multiple personalities, or why others who go through similar traumatic events in their lives do not develop such mental divisions. But the fact is that Christine Costner experienced events in her life that caused her, as she later would say, to develop "coping mechanisms" as "something [she] did to cope with reality."

In May 1937, when Christine was ten years old, her nineteen-year-old uncle, Ernest Hasting, died of pneumonia after a brief illness at Star Fort CCC Camp in Greenwood, South Carolina, a few miles from her home. He was buried in the cemetery of Mount Carmel United Methodist Church in Edgefield, where most of Christine's relatives would find their final resting places.

When Christine was seventeen, her younger sister, Frances, died in infancy in late September 1944. Christine would not remember this until years later, when she was taken to the cemetery and shown her sister's grave. Christine also had two other sisters, Elise and Louise Costner, who were twins.

In about 1951, when she was twenty-three, Christine sought the help of Dr. Thigpen to help resolve the unexplainable events that were plaguing her life. Reportedly, she was referred to him by her own physician. Thigpen also enlisted the aid of his colleague Hervey Cleckley. Her uncontrollable mental problems led to the breakup of her first marriage (1948–1952), to George Rodgers, who came from the tiny community of Ward, South Carolina, not far from Edgefield. Christine would later say, "I don't blame him. It was hard for him to understand that I could turn into a completely different person and do things the other personality would never do." That marriage produced a daughter, Taffy.

On December 19, 1954, she married her second husband, Don Sizemore, who supported his wife not only through the "three faces of Eve" but also through other personalities that eventually emerged. Sizemore, a native of Bear Creek, North Carolina, was an electrician and a navy veteran of World War II. He and Christine had one son, Bobby.

"Never has a man been so patient and understanding as this man," Christine would later say of her husband. "We had a lot of happy times, but there were more trying times during those years and he never complained. . . . I feel my complete cure was due to his love for me." Bobby Sizemore also credits his father with getting the family through the troubled times when his mother was having so many mental problems. He said, "I give my sister and father all the credit in dealing with the situation. My sister raised me many times and deserves the majority of the credit for the way the family dealt with [the situation]."

Of his mother's several personalities, his favorite was the "Retrace Lady," who would go miles out of her way to avoid retracing her steps. He called that personality "the one I considered my truest mother as I was growing up." The one he hated the most was the "Strawberry Girl." Bobby said he once left his mother in a grocery store and later returned to find that the Strawberry Girl had taken her place and had filled more than three shopping carts with every strawberry-flavored food item she could find in the store.

Even before *The Three Faces of Eve* was published, Hollywood was chomping at the bit to turn it into a motion picture. Nunnally Johnson had seen the galley proofs of the book before publication and immediately decided to take on the project as producer, director, and screenwriter. He supposedly is the one who convinced the doctors to call the book *The Three Faces of Eve*. Thigpen said he made three requests to Johnson: that the actors not use fake southern accents; that a couch not be used in the psychiatrists' office; and that the psychiatrists be made human. The role of Eve went to a virtually unknown actress— Joanne Woodward.

British actor Alistair Cooke was cast as the narrator of the movie, with David Wayne playing Eve White's supportive husband. Portraying Cleckley and Thigpen were Lee J. Cobb as "Dr. Curtis Luther" and Edwin Jerome as "Dr. Francis Day." Vince Edwards, who would later become famous as Dr. Ben Casey in the television series *Ben Casey*, portrayed an army sergeant and did not even get name credit.

There is a scene in *The Three Faces of Eve* in which fun-girl personality Eve Black dances and sings for Camp Gordon soldiers. That scene was based on a real-life performance by Christine at the old Club Royal, then located just across the Fifth Street bridge in North Augusta, South Carolina. The Club Royal, a concrete and wood building, burned in 1957, the same year the movie came out. Christine Costner Sizemore would later recall of the club: "It was huge, and it was nice. I was surprised they let me sing there. Eve Black, though, had a nice voice. What I find interesting is that I can't carry a tune in a bucket, but she sang so well. And, if she just appeared there as a guest, they would ask her to sing. She loved it, you know."

On September 18, 1957, the world premiere of *The Three Faces of Eve* was held in the Miller Theater in the 700 block of Broad Street in Augusta. The 2,500-seat art deco–style theater had been built in 1940 for $500,000 by Frank James Miller Sr., who had been a program boy and usher at the Grand Opera House a few blocks away.

The main events started with the "authors' dinner," attended by more than four hundred guests. It began at 6:30 p.m. in the Bon Air Hotel and raised $4,000 for the University Hospital board. Cleckley and Thigpen were presented with gold plaques signed by the president of 20th Century Fox, who thanked them "in recognition and appreciation of your service to the movie industry and the whole world." The VIP guests were then driven to the Miller Theater, about two miles away, in brand-new "snazzy" Edsel automobiles.

The day after the premiere, *The Augusta Chronicle* reported:

A light rain began falling before Zero Hour, but that failed to dampen the spirit of a large crowd that began forming in front of the Miller. The crowd waited patiently until the celebrities began arriving from a patron's banquet at the Bon Air Hotel. The long wait was worth it, the onlookers agreed, when Jody Shattuck, the stunning Miss Georgia, reached the theater at 8:27 p.m. Jody flashed her "Miss Georgia" smile at the crowd, and, after that, nobody gave a second thought to the shower.

Among those absent from the world premiere was the subject of the movie itself. She would later explain: "My therapist at that time, Dr. Corbett Thigpen, who wrote the book on which the movie is based, told me not to. And he told me never to tell anybody I was Eve. He said, if I did, my children wouldn't be able to go to school and my husband would lose his job. I like to believe that he was trying to protect me. There was such a stigma attached to mental illness. A mental patient could be treated like a leper." Christine says that she never saw the movie until about twenty years later, when it was broadcast on television.

In 1970 the Sizemore family moved to Fairfax, Virginia, where Christine continued her therapy with psychiatrist Tony Tsitos. She claimed that about twenty-two personalities would emerge before she finally stabilized with her "normal" personalities. She currently lives in Florida.

In late 1974, Christine accepted an invitation by her twin sisters to speak to their college classes about her illness. As Christine recalled:

> I told them I didn't know how to speak before an audience, that I'd been isolated all my life. But to be honest, that wasn't my greatest fear. No one besides my family and my therapist knew I was Eve. I was afraid of the rejection I might face from people. I talked with Dr. Tsitos about it, and he told me, "Be prepared for rejection, because the world doesn't necessarily love a mental patient. But it's better to do that than to go through the rest of your life scared to death that somebody's going to find out."

When Christine showed up at Piedmont Technical College in Greenwood, South Carolina, she was expecting talk to about fifteen students. Instead, about six hundred people were in the audience, including several media representatives, such as Tom Harrison of *The Augusta Chronicle.* The subhead on Harrison's article on Christine's talk read: "Once she faced life with three personalities; now she faces it with 'acceptance.'" Later, Christine spoke about her coming-out: "It [the lecture] really wasn't planned. I merely walked in unaware, and when I saw all the people and photographers I couldn't walk out."

Her coming-out ultimately led to her 1977 autobiography, *I'm Eve,* as well as numerous speaking engagements as an advocate of mental health. By 2007, the fiftieth anniversary of the movie premiere of *The Three Faces of Eve,* the Miller Theater in Augusta had long been closed. But Mike Deas, a board member of the historic Imperial Theatre across Broad Street, decided to reenact the premiere that Christine had missed.

So Deas created an incredibly memorable night for Christine. She was driven to the front of the theater to greet adoring fans and to see a screening of the movie that had made her world famous. Unfortunately, her wonderfully supportive husband, Don Sizemore, was not there with her, having died on August 16, 1992, at the Department of Veterans Affairs Medical Center in Columbia, South Carolina. He was sixty-nine. Sizemore was buried in the cemetery of Mount Carmel United Methodist Church in Edgefield, where members of the Costner family lie and where Christine herself expects to be interred one day.

"Just like you have memories of your past, I have memories of mine, now," Christine told me in 2007. "But when I was ill, I didn't know what the others [personalities] were doing. But once the healing took place, I retained all the memories."

"Is there still some Eve Black left in Christine Costner Sizemore?" I asked.

Christine replied, "Of course. I enjoy having fun, but I'm like everybody else, now. There is a part of me that enjoys fun, and there is a serious part like being a mother. There are so many people that don't know how to relax anymore. They're so serious about life and everything that goes with it that they really don't know how to live."

Christine seems to have finally come to grips with who she really is, unlike many people with personal problems.

"And I think that's sad," she added, "because what else is there in our life except recognizing ourselves and living to the fullest of our abilities every day?"

I asked whether she had ever crossed paths with Joanne Woodward, who portrayed her so well in the movie. She replied, "No, but I have met [actor and car racer] Paul Newman. I used to go to car races when I lived in Fairfax, Virginia. I was there with my girlfriends, when they urged me to go up and speak to him. So I went up to him and said, 'I'm Eve.' He pushed his sunglasses on top of his head and said, 'I'm Adam.'"

At the fiftieth anniversary of the movie's premiere, it seemed only fitting that I give Christine something special—something that had come into my possession thirty-five years earlier when I interviewed Augusta psychiatrists Hervey Cleckley and Corbett Thigpen on the twentieth anniversary of their presentation to the American Psychiatric Association in 1953.

The two doctors had surprised me with a copy of their original paper, "A Case of Multiple Personality," which they had presented in Los Angeles and which I had them autograph. And who deserved it more? Surely that would be the person who had never before seen a copy of that very personal paper: Christine Costner Sizemore, the one and only face behind *The Three Faces of Eve*.

CHAPTER 3

JOHN ROSS, CHIEF OF THE CHEROKEES

What if the U.S. Congress ordered all Chinese Americans living in California to give up their comfortable houses, rich agricultural land, and means of livelihood and relocate to the Ozark hills in Missouri? What if Congress ordered all black citizens in Georgia and South Carolina to give up their familiar lives and relocate to the deserts of Nevada or the plains of North Dakota?

In truth, that is exactly what the U.S. Congress did in 1830 in passing the Indian Removal Act, which authorized President Andrew Jackson to designate lands west of the Mississippi River in "exchange" for Indian lands in the eastern part of the country. It didn't matter that thousands of Native Americans did not want to move from their ancestral territories. The U.S. government urgently wanted to relocate them. Why? Because, as the nation began to expand from the original thirteen colonies before and after the Revolutionary War, white pioneers wanted the Indians' rich soil, especially after that soil revealed veins of gold in north Georgia.

Just as remarkable as the story of how the U.S. government removed the Indians from the eastern southern states is the story of John Ross, a Scottish American born in Alabama. He barely knew Indian dialect, yet he was chief of the Cherokee nation for nearly forty years and led fifteen thousand Cherokees in their relocation from Georgia to Oklahoma on what became known as the Trail of Tears.

The mystery lies in answering a couple of questions: How did Ross become elevated to such a historical status? And why was he a crusader for the Cherokee people?

Various sources say that a Scotsman named William Shorey took as his wife Ghigooie, a Cherokee of the Bird Clan. Their daughter, Anna, in 1769 married John McDonald, near Fort Loudoun, Tennessee, a British fort south of Knoxville. McDonald was born in the Scottish Highlands near Inverness. John and Anna McDonald had a daughter named Mollie, who in 1786 married a Scotsman named Daniel Ross, a trader who had gone to live among the Cherokees during the American Revolution. The union of Daniel and Mollie Ross produced their son John Ross, born on October 3, 1790, in Turkey Town, Alabama, near the present town of Center, along the Coosa River near Lookout Mountain.

As part Cherokee, John Ross was immersed in the Cherokee culture of the area but was educated by English-speaking people, including the Reverend Gideon Blackburn. When he became an adult, he also assumed the Cherokee name of Kooweskoowe, a rare and possibly mythological bird.

By the age of twenty, Ross was involved in trading with the U.S. government in the area of Georgia that became known as Rossville, just south of the Georgia-Tennessee border. He apparently also served as postmaster of Rossville. After the death of his mother, Ross in 1808 moved into his grandfather's two-story, log-built home. Ross would live in this house until he sold it to a relative in 1827. It would pass down through several owners until it eventually became a public historic site and the oldest remaining structure in northwest Georgia.

In 1802, when Ross was about twelve, the Georgia General Assembly signed a compact giving the U.S. government all of Georgia's claims to western lands in exchange for the federal government's pledge to invalidate all Indian titles to land within the state. This predatory attitude of Georgia pioneers had begun almost half a century earlier. On November 10, 1763, in Augusta, after the British royal governors of the colonies of Georgia, Virginia, North Carolina, and South Carolina met with about eight hundred Indians representing the Creeks, Cherokees, Choctaws, Catawbas, and Chickasaws, the various parties signed a treaty that resulted in forfeiting Indian land. A plaque on the side of St. Paul's Episcopal Church at Sixth and Reynolds Streets commemorates this significant gathering.

As Edward J. Cashin, chairman of the Augusta State University history department, writes in his book *Story of Augusta*,

"The most important part of the treaty for the town of Augusta [later to be Georgia's capital for ten years] was the agreement to permit the English to settle as far above Augusta as the Little River and as far west as the Ogeechee River. The line was not actually surveyed until 1768, nor did it contain the restless squatters for very long. Even [Georgia] Governor Wright ignored the line when he granted lands outside its limits in 1771."

John Ross's involvement with the government led him to join up with the American forces led by General Andrew Jackson in fighting the British-allied Creeks. He held the rank of lieutenant during the War of 1812 and fought in the battle of Horseshoe Bend in central Alabama in the spring of 1814.

General Jackson's forces of about 3,300 men included a west Tennessee militia, the Thirty-ninth U.S. Infantry, and Indians of the Cherokee, Choctaw, and Lower Creek tribes. They fought against about a thousand Upper Creek warriors at a bend on the Tallapoosa River. About fifty U.S. soldiers and more than eight hundred Upper Creeks (known as Red Sticks) died in the battle. It is said that the conflict represented the worst loss of Native American warriors in a single battle. Today the battle site, sixty-eight miles north of Montgomery, is a 2,040-acre national park.

Following the defeat, Jackson forced all Creeks to sign the Treaty of Fort Jackson on August 9, 1814, ignoring the fact that he had won the battle with the help of Lower Creeks. As a result of the treaty, the Creeks had to turn over roughly twenty-three million acres in Alabama and Georgia to the U.S. government. Jackson's success at the battle of Horseshoe Bend, coupled with his victory at the battle of New Orleans against the British, propelled him onto the national stage.

John Ross, meanwhile, returned to the area of northwestern Georgia where he owned slaves; engaged in several businesses, including farming some 170 acres; maintained a warehouse; and operated a ferryboat at Ross's Landing, which evolved into the present-day city of Chattanooga. He married Elizabeth Brown Henley (also known as Quatie), who was part Cherokee and who had a daughter from a previous marriage. Together, John and Quatie Ross had three sons and a daughter who would grow to adulthood, as well as a child who died in infancy.

It also was about this time that John Ross began entering the world of politics, defending Cherokees against encroachments by the state and federal governments and handling other financial and political matters. His ability to speak English, coupled with his extensive educational background, made him a valuable and respected leader. He had the support of Principal Cherokee Chief Pathkiller, Associate Chief Charles R. Hicks, and elder Cherokee statesman Major Ridge, and served as a clerk for the less-well-educated Pathkiller and Hicks.

His first important venture into national politics took place in 1816, when the Cherokee National Council named Ross to be part of a delegation to Washington, D.C., sent to resolve increasing problems of territorial boundaries and whites' intrusions on Cherokee land. Apparently, Ross was the only member of the delegation who was fluent in English, making him a key player on the trip. The following year Ross joined the Cherokee National Council and served as its president from 1819 to 1826.

In 1819 Ross made a second journey to Washington, D.C., to clarify a treaty of 1817. That trip would prove eventful. Because of a rivalry that had developed between Ross and a Cherokee chief named John Walker Jr., Walker tried unsuccessfully to kill Ross with a knife during the trip. Their feud continued to escalate over the years. In 1834 Walker's son, John Walker III, was assassinated by Ross's political supporters.

Like Ross Walker owned a ferry-crossing business, with his being on the Hiawassee River in McMinn County, Tennessee, at present-day Calhoun. Also like Ross, Walker had a white father and an Indian mother. Walker, however, sided with the federal government on the question of removal of Indians from territory sought by the U.S. government—perhaps because in 1819 the U.S. government granted Walker two large 640-acre tracts. One tract included his home and ferry business, while the other contained his gristmills and sawmills.

Secretary of War John C. Calhoun increasingly pressured Ross and other Cherokee leaders to cede to the federal government tracts of land in Georgia and Tennessee. The pressure reached such a level that in January 1824 Calhoun made two offers to the Cherokees: Either turn over title to their lands and move westward, or accept denationalization and become citizens of the United States.

Three months later, rather than accepting either choice, Ross did something unheard of: He directly petitioned Congress to consider the Cherokees' grievances. The fact that "savages" were able to argue legal points as well as most whites caused politicians not only in Washington but also in other parts of the nation to take notice.

The Cherokees decided that the best defense in fighting the U.S. government was to create their own structured government, with John Ross as their leader. The Cherokee National Council adopted a series of laws creating a bicameral national government and a Cherokee Supreme Court in 1822. A twenty-four-member constitutional committee, of which Ross was a member, drafted a constitution calling for a principal chief and other governmental bodies.

The Cherokee national legislature was formed on November 12, 1825, and a capital named New Echota was established at the headwaters of the Oostanaula River. At New Echota, a Cherokee named Sequoyah created a written language for Cherokees. It consisted of eighty-six characters and was used in the *Cherokee Phoenix*, a bilingual newspaper printed in New Echota.

Strangely, in January 1827, about ten months before the new Cherokee constitution was ratified, both Principal Chief Pathkiller and Associate Chief Charles R. Hicks died. The constitution did not take effect until October 1828, at which time John "Kooweskoowe" Ross became the first constitutional principal chief and official leader of the Cherokee nation. This was the same John Ross whose paternal father, grandfather, and other ancestors had been born in Scotland. He would remain the Cherokees' official leader until his death thirty-eight years later.

Many challenges—including the election of Andrew Jackson as president in 1828—awaited the new chief's attention as the U.S. government continued its efforts to push the Cherokees out of Georgia and Tennessee.

Most of the Creeks in Georgia already had been relocated to Oklahoma following a treaty signed in 1827 by Chief McIntosh Jr. McIntosh's father, Captain William McIntosh, was a white man from a prominent family in Savannah, Georgia; his mother, Senoia (or Senoya), was Creek.

The life stories of John Ross and Chief McIntosh held some parallels. Ross was raised among Cherokees; McIntosh was raised among Creeks. Ross distinguished himself at the battle of Horseshoe Bend in the conflict between the Upper and Lower Creeks, as did McIntosh, who was promoted to brigadier general in the U.S. Army. After the War of 1812, Ross built a large plantation in northwest Georgia; McIntosh built his plantation, with more than seventy slaves, on the Chattahoochee River in Carroll County, about thirty-five miles southwest of present-day Atlanta.

For whatever reasons, McIntosh on February 12, 1825, joined eight other Creek chiefs in signing the Treaty of Indian

Springs (near Jackson, forty miles south of present-day Atlanta), exchanging the remaining Creeks' land in Georgia for $400,000. In effect, McIntosh had signed his own death sentence. Just before daybreak on April 30, 1827, about two hundred Creeks descended on the McIntosh plantation and set fire to the home. They stabbed, shot, and scalped McIntosh before throwing his body into the Chattahoochee River.

If any one thing sealed the fate of the Cherokees in Georgia, it was the discovery of gold around Dahlonega, fifty-five miles east of New Echota. Roughly $20 million in gold was mined in the area between 1829 and 1839, and a branch of the U.S. Mint in Dahlonega issued more than $6 million in gold coins between 1838 and 1861. The discovery of gold led to increased efforts to get the Cherokees off land believed to have veins of the precious metal.

In 1827 Chief John Ross left Rossville and moved about fifty miles south. He established a plantation at Coosa (just west of present-day Rome) and operated another ferryboat business, where the Etowah and Oostanaula Rivers meet to form the Coosa River.

Living in the area was Ross's friend and ally Major Ridge, another leader of the Cherokee nation. Ridge had been born in Tennessee with the Indian name Kah-nung-da-tla-geh, meaning "the man who walks on the mountaintop." Therefore, English-speaking settlers called him "The Ridge." Along with Ross and McIntosh, he fought in the battle of Horseshoe Bend in Alabama.

His title of "major" was supposedly given to him by General Andrew Jackson, and for the rest of his life he was known as Major Ridge. He built a log cabin for his family on the banks of the Oostanaula River, where he also operated a ferryboat business. As Ridge's political and business fortunes increased, the house was expanded into a two-story structure with weatherboarding, ceilings, walnut doors, and a carved pine staircase.

On May 26, 1830, President Andrew Jackson, the former Indian fighter, signed the Indian Removal Act. The Twenty-first Congress had passed the bill after bitter debate. Noted dissenters who argued against the removal included Senators Henry Clay of Kentucky, Daniel Webster of Massachusetts, and Theodore Frelinghuysen of New Jersey, and Representatives Ambrose Spencer of New York and David "Davy" Crockett of Tennessee. Crockett, of course, would be killed in 1836 defending the Alamo in Texas.

Supposedly, Daniel Webster and Theodore Frelinghuysen urged Chief Ross and the Cherokee government to select William Wirt to defend Cherokee rights before the U.S. Supreme Court. Wirt had served as attorney general in the administrations of Presidents James Monroe and John Quincy Adams. Wirt argued two cases before the Supreme Court—*Cherokee Nation v. Georgia* and *Worcester v. Georgia*—with both favoring the Cherokees, but that didn't stop President Jackson, who continued to ramrod his efforts to confiscate Cherokee lands for the U.S. government.

Another fatal blow to the Cherokees came with the betrayal by one of Ross's own allies, Chief Major Ridge. The chief, along with his son, John Ridge, and Elias Boudinot, decided that the fight with the U.S. government was hopeless and in 1835 joined other Native American leaders in signing the Treaty of New Echota, which agreed to exchange the Cherokees' ancestral lands for $5.7 million. It didn't matter that the Ridges and Boudinot represented only about five hundred of the seventeen thousand Cherokees left in the state. Chief Ross reportedly obtained sixteen thousand signatures of Cherokees, showing that the Ridge group did not speak for the majority of Cherokees, but that didn't matter to Jackson. On May 23, 1836, Congress eventually ratified, by a single vote, the Treaty of New Echota, setting in motion the gigantic and shameful forced migration known today as the Trail of Tears.

Ross is said to be the author of an emotional appeal in 1836 to the Senate and House of Representatives in a letter now often referred to as "Our Hearts Are Sickened." The letter states in part:

> By the stipulations of this instrument, we are despoiled of our private possessions, the indefeasible property of individuals. We are stripped of every attribute of freedom and eligibility for legal self-defense. Our property may be plundered before our eyes; violence may be committed on our persons; even our lives may be taken away, and there is none to regard our complaints. We are

denationalized; we are disfranchised. We are deprived of membership in the human family! We have neither land nor home, nor resting place that can be called our own. And this is effected by the provisions of a compact which assumes the venerated, the sacred appellation of treaty.

We are overwhelmed! Our hearts are sickened, our utterance is paralyzed, when we reflect on the condition in which we are placed, by the audacious practices of unprincipled men, who have managed their stratagems with so much dexterity as to impose on the Government of the United States, in the face of our earnest, solemn, and reiterated protestations.

We are, indeed, an afflicted people! Our spirits are subdued! Despair has well nigh seized upon our energies! But we speak to the representatives of a Christian country; the friends of justice; the patrons of the oppressed. And our hopes revive, and our prospects brighten, as we indulge the thought. On your sentence, our fate is suspended; prosperity or desolation depends on your word. To you, therefore, we look! Before your august assembly we present ourselves, in the attitude of deprecation, and of entreaty. On your kindness, on your humanity, on your compassion, on your benevolence, we rest our hopes.

To you we address our reiterated prayers. Spare our people! Spare the wreck of our prosperity! Let not our deserted homes become the monuments of our desolation! But we forbear! We suppress the agonies which wring our hearts, when we look at our wives, our children, and our venerable sires! We restrain the forebodings of anguish and distress, of misery and devastation and death, which must be the attendants on the execution of this ruinous compact.

At the direction of the government in Washington, D.C., General Winfield Scott arrived at the Cherokees' capital of New Echota on May 17, 1838, with roughly seven thousand soldiers. The Cherokees who remained in the area had been rounded up into relocation camps around New Echota. Seeing that the situation was hopeless, Chief Ross talked General Scott into letting him organize the roughly fifteen thousand Cherokees being forced to migrate into smaller groups so that they could forage for food while they made the 2,200-mile journey during the winter of 1838–1839.

That action was said to have saved many lives. Nonetheless, the forced migration still resulted in the deaths of about four thousand Cherokee men, women, and children, including Ross's own wife, Quatie, who gave up her blanket to a sick child. She died of pneumonia near Little Rock, Arkansas. A marker there commemorates her death and sacrifice. Ross would continue to be an exalted leader of the Cherokee nation for the rest of his life, while his traitorous former friend and ally, Major Ridge, would become the victim of Cherokee revenge justice.

After signing the Treaty of New Echota and financially benefiting from his Judas-like action, Ridge, his family, and his supporters voluntarily relocated to the new Indian territory in Oklahoma. Ridge allegedly gave his plantation home in Rome, Georgia, to white settlers. It would pass through several owners before being acquired by the Junior League. Today it is a Georgia historic site known also as the Chieftains Museum.

On June 22, 1839, reportedly upon official direction of Cherokee leaders or possibly at the order of Chief Ross's supporters, it was payback time. At daybreak Ridge's son, John, was dragged from his bed by Cherokees, pulled into his front yard, and stabbed to death in front of his wife and children. A few hours later, Major Ridge was attacked while riding toward a nearby town and was shot and stabbed to death. And that same morning, fellow traitor Elias Boudinot was lured from his house on the premise that he was needed to help obtain some medical supplies. He was stabbed and tomahawked to death.

During the Civil War years, Chief Ross unfortunately steered his people to siding with the Confederate government, thinking that such an alliance would lead to the restoration of Cherokee national rights and the possible return to the Cherokees' ancestral land. The Union army, however, invaded the Cherokee nation in July 1862. In 1863 Union troops burned Ross's two-story, white-column, southern-style mansion at Park Hill, Oklahoma. Contrary to what so many Americans erroneously believed, he and his fellow Creek and Cherokee chiefs were not living in tepees or wigwams. In keeping with their elevated political status and business success, they lived in comfortable homes like the white settlers.

Throughout the Civil War and afterward, Ross continued to make trips to Washington, D.C., to fight with legal means rather than physical weapons for his beloved people. He was on such a mission when he died in his bed at the Medes Hotel on August 1, 1866. His body was returned to Park Hill, where his grave today is marked by a tall tombstone in the Ross family cemetery.

Most Americans probably have never heard of this Scottish American who championed the Cherokees' cause all of his life and who served as their chief for almost forty years. But in the hearts and minds of Cherokee Americans, John Ross always will remain a legend.

CHAPTER 4

PREACHER'S CURSE ON JACKSONBOROUGH

In eastern Georgia near the border with South Carolina, there used to exist a booming town called Jacksonborough, located four miles north of Sylvania and about halfway between Augusta and Savannah. For more than forty years in the late 1700s and early 1800s, the town was even the official seat of government for Screven County. But today there are almost no traces of the once-growing populace except for a lone two-story house that was built in 1815 and restored in the late 1960s. Yet some say that on starlit, moon-filled nights you can hear the sounds of the once-raucous residents partying into the early morning hours, shooting off their guns, and yelling at the top of their lungs.

So what happened to Jacksonborough and its residents? Some say that its very strange and mysterious disappearance just came with time and changing migration patterns. But others who believe in curses and religious faith attribute it to the despicable ways that the town's godless people treated a famous visiting evangelist.

Originally, the area was inhabited by Yuchi Indians, who themselves had their own mysterious ways of calling up the spirits to deal with their enemies. Starting in 1751, they were joined by German immigrants, who settled many of the towns in Georgia and South Carolina.

On March 3, 1779, the area became the scene of an important battle of the Revolutionary War, when a large contingent of British soldiers defeated a much smaller band of Georgia militia and Continental soldiers. The British expected to crush the Americans easily, but it turned out to be a hard-fought victory, with heavy casualties on both sides. According to a Georgia Historical Commission marker at the battle site, "So fiercely did these Georgians fight that the British had to bring up reserves. Asking no quarter, they fought until nearly every man was dead or wounded. . . . Thus ended, in disaster, the well laid plans [of the British] to win control of the South and bring the war to an end. Only the matchless bravery of the Georgians in the last stand gave solace and inspiration in an almost hopeless situation."

On his tour of the South, one of the greatest figures of the Revolutionary War, George Washington, spent the night of May 16, 1791, lodging in the area at the inn of Stephen Calfrey Pearce near the present-day town of Farmdale, twelve miles southeast of Sylvania. Two years later, on December 14, 1793, the Georgia General Assembly created Screven County, Georgia's fourteenth, from parts of Burke and Effingham Counties. The county was

DON RHODES

The town of Jacksonborough was incorporated by the Georgia General Assembly in 1799. The spelling informally changed to Jacksonboro over the years, as this Georgia Historical Commission marker notes.

named for Revolutionary War General James Screven, who was mortally wounded in 1778 during a skirmish with the British on Spencer Hill near Midway, Georgia, south of Savannah.

On February 1, 1797, the Georgia General Assembly passed an act establishing the town of Jacksonborough as the county seat of Screven County. The town, named for then Governor James Jackson, was to be built next to Beaver Dam Creek on fifty acres purchased from Samuel and Mary Gross. It quickly prospered, with inhabitants shipping their crops and other goods down the nearby Savannah River to the equally prospering port city of Savannah.

Everything was going just fine until the visit of Lorenzo Dow, a Methodist evangelist, in 1820. To most people of his day, Dow was a really strange bird, and yet he was said to be the Billy Graham of his time, preaching to as many as ten thousand people at some assemblies. At one time, his autobiography reportedly was the second-best-selling book in the United States, second only to the Bible. Dow was born in Coventry, Connecticut, near Hartford, on October 16, 1777, and became a circuit-riding preacher in 1798. He mainly followed the doctrine of the Methodist church, although he was never officially connected with the Methodist ministry. In 1799 and 1805 he made trips to Ireland and England, where he was greeted by immense crowds fascinated as much by his eccentric ways as by his eloquent oratory. He also traveled throughout Canada and the United States and made one trip to the West Indies.

His long, unkempt hair was parted in the middle, and he wore the clothes on his thin body until they were in tatters. He never carried luggage and mostly walked on his journeys of thousands of miles. All that he carried were boxes of Bibles, which he would give away. He was known to appear unannounced at public events and shout in a loud voice that he would return exactly one year from that day to preach in the same place. And sure enough, 365 days later, he would return to deliver his sermon. He was a fierce opponent of Roman Catholicism, and like John Wesley, the founder of Methodism, Dow was a vocal opponent of slavery, a stance that did not make him a popular figure in the pre–Civil War southern states. Frequently he was physically attacked, but still he courageously walked from town to town in the South with his Gospel messages. He reportedly delivered the first Protestant sermons in Alabama in 1803 and 1804 and lured a crowd of five thousand people to one camp meeting held not far from Jacksonborough.

So his fame and moral positions certainly were already known when Lorenzo Dow walked into Jacksonborough to preach against the evils of drinking and slavery and other things that the rowdy residents didn't want to hear. In fact, by that time the town had earned a widespread reputation as a violent, almost out-of-control place, with the bad folks pretty much outnumbering the good.

Clyde Hollingsworth, the late Screven County historian and editor of *The Sylvania Telephone* newspaper, wrote an account of Dow's memorable visit that was often repeated by generations of county residents. Hollingsworth said that when Dow came to Jacksonborough around 1821, he immediately walked about town passing out printed notices of a sermon he would be giving at the local Methodist church. He was a guest at the home of Seaborn Goodall, clerk of the Screven County Superior Court, who also had served as postmaster of Jacksonborough. According to Hollingsworth, it was Goodall who introduced Dow at the Methodist church gathering. But just as Dow began talking, the quiet evening and solemn occasion was interrupted by drunken men outside the church who shot off their pistols, tossed rocks through the open windows, and did everything else they could to prevent Dow from continuing his sermon.

According to Hollingsworth, "Dow left the church in a rage and shadowed his disturbers until they returned to one of the saloons. He then charged into the saloon alone, seized an iron tool, broke in the head of a barrel of whiskey and overturned its contents on the floor before the amazed customers of the bar could stop him." Hollingsworth said that they immediately jumped on Dow and began beating him unmercifully until his benefactor and host Seaborn Goodall came to his rescue, took Dow back to Goodall's house, and treated the preacher's bruises and wounds.

As the partially hunchbacked Dow was walking out of town to his next evangelistic opportunity, some men of Jacksonborough seized the thin preacher, laid him down between two wide boards like meat in a sandwich, and sat on him, saying they would help straighten him out while they laughed and shouted insults at him. Dow managed to escape his tormentors and crossed the nearby bridge over Beaver Dam Creek. However, he was not finished with Jacksonborough and its evil ways. "Effecting a return of his dignity and ecclesiastical manner," said Hollingsworth, "he dramatically stamped the dust from his feet and pronounced a curse on the town, asking God to destroy it excepting only the home of Mr. Goodall."

Say what you will about such curses, whether they come from witches or preachers, but it wasn't long before Jacksonborough's houses and businesses began deteriorating and disappearing because of unexplained fires, ferocious tornadoes, lightning storms, and other calamities. The usually peaceful Beaver Dam Creek turned into a raging waterway that caused flash floods and destroyed crops as well as buildings. Year by year, the town's population began moving away, and in 1847 the Georgia General Assembly moved the county seat from Jacksonborough to Sylvania.

Evangelist Dow could not have known that his curse apparently had come to pass and was sealed by the removal of the county seat, for in 1834 he died in Georgetown, District of Columbia, and was buried in Oak Hill Cemetery in Washington, D.C. But if you travel south on US 301 and look to your right in the curve just south of the intersection with GA 24, you will see a large sign pointing to a two-story house restored by the Brier Creek Chapter of the Daughters of the American Revolution and now listed on the National Register of Historic Places. And who formerly owned the only structure that survives from the once-booming town of Jacksonborough? Why, none other than Seaborn Goodall, who gave shelter and comfort to Lorenzo Dow.

CHAPTER 5

JIMMY CARTER AND THE UFO

By 1969, long before he became president of the United States, James Earl Carter Jr. was already becoming well known as a respected leader across the state of Georgia, having been elected to the state's senate in 1962 and having made an unsuccessful bid for governor in 1966.

He was about two years away from finally becoming governor of Georgia and almost seven years away from becoming president when he went to the tiny town of Leary in southwestern Georgia in his capacity as district governor of the Lions Club. His father had been a founding member of the Lions Club in Plains, Georgia.

As Carter would later disclose, he and several members of the Leary Lions Club were standing outside about 7:15 p.m., shortly after dark, when something unusual caught Carter's eyes about 30 degrees above the horizon. He described it as "bright as [the] moon" and said that it was bluish at first and then became reddish. In the ten to twelve minutes that he watched the object,

Georgia Governor Jimmy Carter, later United States president, so firmly believed that he had seen an unidentified flying object that he filed an official report about his observations.

it seemed to come toward the town and then stopped and moved "partially away" before returning and finally departing.

Carter said that the unexplained incident took place in October 1969, but researchers who checked with International Lions Club records apparently proved that Carter spoke to the Leary Lions Club on January 6, 1969, and that this club had actually been disbanded by the following October.

Either way, the matter stayed on Carter's mind after he

became governor. He was in Statesboro, Georgia, home of Georgia Southern University, in September 1973, when he was asked at a press conference about several recent sightings of unidentified flying objects in the state. He surprised those present by contending that he himself had a similar experience and told of his sighting in Leary four years earlier.

Instead of backing down from his public disclosure, Carter took an even more unusual step for an elected public official: On September 18, 1973, he filled out a form from the International UFO Bureau in Oklahoma City, Oklahoma, in his own handwriting and mailed it back. His answers to the form's questions appear below.

1. Name: *Jimmy Carter*
Address: *State Capitol Atlanta*
Telephone: *404-656-1776*
Occupation: *Governor*
Special Training: *Nuclear Physics*
Military Service: *U.S. Navy*

2. Date of Observation: *October 1969*
Time: *7:15 p.m. E.S.T.*

3. Locality of Observation: *Leary, Georgia*

4. How long did you see the object? Hours: *10–12 minutes.* Seconds: *[Left blank]*

5. Please describe weather conditions and the type of sky; i.e., bright daylight, nighttime, dusk, etc. *Shortly after dark*

6. Position of the Sun or Moon in relation to the object and to you: *Not visible*

7. If seen at night, twilight, or dawn, were the stars or moon visible? *Stars*

8. [Was] there more than one object? *No*

9. Please describe the object(s) in detail. *[Left blank]*

10. Was the object(s) brighter than the background of the sky? *Yes*

11. If so, compare the brightness with the Sun, Moon, headlights, etc. *At one time, as bright as moon.*

12. Did the object(s):
A. Appear to stand still at any time? *Yes*
B. Suddenly speed up and rush away at any time? *[Left blank]*
C. Break up into two parts or explode? *[Left blank]*
D. Give off smoke? *[Left blank]*
E. Leave any visible trail? *[Left blank]*

F. Drop anything? *[Left blank]*

G. Change brightness? **Yes**

H. Change shape? **Yes**

I . Change color? **Yes, seemed to move toward us from a distance, stop, move partially away, return, then depart, bluish at first, then reddish, luminous, not solid.**

13. Did object(s) at any time pass in front of, or behind anything? If so, please elaborate giving distance, size, etc., if possible. **No**

14. Was there any wind? **No**

15. Did you observe the object(s) through an optical instrument or other aid, windshield, window pane, storm window, screening, etc.? What? **No**

16. Did the object(s) have any sound? **No**

17. Please tell if the object(s) were:

A. Fuzzy or blurred. *[Left blank]*

B. Like a bright star. *[Left blank]*

C. Sharply outlined. ✓ *[Carter made a check mark]*

18. Was the object:

A. Self luminous? ✓

B. Dull finish? *[Left blank]*

C. Reflecting? *[Left blank]*

D. Transparent? *[Left blank]*

Notice: Please draw, to the best of your ability, a sketch of the object(s), including all details. You may use extra sheet. *[Left blank]*

19. Did the object(s) rise or fall while in motion? ***Came close, moved away, came close, then moved away.***

20. Tell the apparent size of the object when compared with the following held at length. Pinhead, pea, etc. ***[Carter checked none of the choices but wrote:] About same as moon, maybe a little smaller. Varied from brighter/larger than planet to apparent size of moon.***

21. How did you happen to notice the object(s)? ***10–12 men all watched it. Brightness attracted us.***

22. Where were you and what were you doing at the time? ***Outdoors waiting for a meeting to begin at 7:30 p.m.***

23. How did the object(s) disappear from view? ***Moved to distance then disappeared.***

24. Compare the speed of the object(s) with a piston or jet aircraft at the same apparent altitude. *Not pertinent.*

25. Were there any conventional aircraft in the location at the time or immediately afterward? *No*

26. Please estimate the distance of the object(s). *Difficult. Maybe 300–1,000 yards.*

27. What was the elevation of the object(s) in the sky? *About 30 degrees above the horizon.*

28. Names and addresses of other witnesses, if any: *10 members of Leary, Ga., Lions Club.*

29. Please draw a map of the locality of the observation showing North, the direction from which the object(s) appeared and disappeared from view; the direction of its course over the area; roads, towns, villages, railroads, and other landmarks within a mile. *Appeared from west about 30 degrees up.*

30. Is there an airport, military, governmental, or research installation in the area? *No*

31. Have you seen other objects of an unidentified nature? *No*

32. Please enclose photographs, motion pictures, news-paper clippings. *[Carter drew line to indicate not applicable]*

33. Were you interrogated by Air Forces investigators? **No.** Were you asked or told not to reveal or discuss the incident? If so . . . *No*

34. We would like your permission to quote your name in connection with this report. . . . However if you prefer, we will keep your name confidential. . . . Please note your choice by checking the proper statement below:

You may use my name. ✓ *[Amazingly, Carter placed a check mark here]*

Please keep my name confidential.

Date of filling out this report: *9/18/73*

Signature:

Jimmy Carter

Much to his credit, Carter did not deny his original remarks about the UFO. Moreover, he continued to talk about his experience even when the mayor of Leary, Georgia, and other club members supposedly denied having seen the object and even when "UFO experts" maintained that Carter was confusing the UFO with the planet Venus, as others had done. Carter responded that he was an amateur astronomer and definitely knew the difference. Later, in his capacity as president of the United States, he would also say that he knew of no government cover-up regarding UFOs and that he himself did not believe extraterrestrials had ever visited Earth.

In an article by Wil S. Hylton in the December 2005 issue of *GQ* magazine, Carter was quoted as saying:

> I saw an unidentified flying object. I've never believed that it came from Mars. I know enough physics to know that you can't have vehicles that are tangible in nature flying from Mars, looking around, and then flying back. But I saw an object one night when I was preparing to give a speech to a Lions Club.
>
> There were about twenty-five of us men standing around. It was almost time for the Lions Club supper to start, which I would eat and then I would give a speech. I was in charge of fifty-six Lions Clubs in south-west Georgia back in the late '60s. And all of a sudden, one of the men looked up and said, "Look, over in the west!" And there was a bright light in the sky. We all saw it. And then the light, it got closer and closer to us. And then it stopped, I don't know how far away, but it stopped beyond the pine trees. And all of a sudden it changed color to blue, and then it changed to red, then back to white. And we were trying to figure out what

in the world it could be, and then it receded into the distance.

I had a tape recorder—because as I met with members of Lions Clubs, I would dictate their names on the tapes so I could remember them—and I dictated my observations. And when I got home, I wrote them down. So that's an accurate description of what I saw. It was a flying object that was unidentified. But I have never thought that it was from outer space.

One of the earliest UFO sightings was reported by textile mill employee Jack Reames of Bath, South Carolina, on the Savannah River at the Georgia border. Reames told *The Augusta Chronicle* that he was leaving his house about 10:25 p.m. on June 30, 1947, when he happened to look into the sky and saw a single, flat disc flying about thirty yards above the hill on which his house was located. As the *Chronicle* reported on its front page:

> He described the disc as being about 12 inches in diameter, looking like aluminum and giving off a small amount of light. He said that the disc was traveling at a speed that he would be unable to estimate but said that it was going so fast that it disappeared in a few seconds. There was only one disc, and it was traveling in a northerly direction, he declared.
>
> Mr. Reames said that he had never seen anything like it. Explaining that he had seen the Arctic northern

lights while he was stationed as a sergeant in the field artillery in Iceland and that he had often observed falling stars, he pointed out that the phenomena that he witnessed could not be explained by saying that they were northern lights or falling stars. He said there were no clouds to reflect any light from the ground and no airport or buildings that could give off enough light to be reflected.

More local reports followed. On July 5 the *Chronicle* reported on its front page that a prominent Augusta physician, Colden Battey, had seen "flying saucers" six weeks earlier. Battey saw the objects about 11:00 a.m. while he was fishing off St. Helena Sound near Beaufort, South Carolina (between Charleston and Savannah). Battey told the *Chronicle* that the four discs were flying at more than 20,000 feet altitude at a "terrific" rate of speed.

The *Chronicle* noted: "He described the 'saucers' as seeming at that altitude about six inches in diameter and about one inch thick. He said they looked silver and 'highly polished.' He said that the discs had a projection or rim around them about one-quarter distance from their edges."

Battey said he had refrained from mentioning them publicly because he was under the impression they were meteorological balloons or "some new type of flying wing aircraft." On July 6, 1947, the day after the article about Battey, the *Chronicle* published a huge front-page headline that proclaimed: "'Flying Saucer' Mystery Baffles Entire Country; Explanation Is Lacking."

The subheads below the main headline read: "Government Sheds No Light on Puzzle" and "Strange Discs Now Reported in 31 States; VFW Chief Says He's Expecting Information."

That article included the following:

"We realize," said Dr. Oliver Lee, director of Northwestern University's Dearborn Observatory, "that the army and navy are working on all sorts of things we know nothing about."

Lee said the discs might represent the same sort of thing as sending radar signals to the moon, "one of the greatest technological achievements of the war and accomplished in absolute secrecy."

In July 1964 the Associated Press reported that Beauford E. Parham of Wellford, South Carolina, was traveling from Atlanta on the night of June 29 near Lavonia, Georgia, not far from the South Carolina state line, when a circular flying object came hissing down and "stopped in the air like a humming bird" over his car. He claimed that it blistered the paint on his car and burned his arm. Parham was quoted as saying, "I saw it so clearly I believe I could build one of the things."

Hmmmm, doesn't that sound like a scene out of the movie *Close Encounters of the Third Kind?*

In the mid-1960s many sightings of UFOs over Georgia were reported. Here is one *The Augusta Chronicle* published Thursday, February 16, 1967:

"I'm not a nut, but . . ."

With that a 41-year-old woman from Augusta described a weird, orange light that kept pace with her car on U.S. 1 south of Augusta Wednesday night.

It was the second unidentified flying object report telephoned to *The Chronicle* office between 11 and 11:30 p.m. Both reports placed the object between Augusta and Wrens [Georgia]. The woman said the object glowed brightly with an orange light that clearly outlined trees beside the highway. She said it finally "just disappeared."

The object kept pace with her car for about five minutes, she said, before "it just wasn't there any more."

She estimated that she was between 10 to 20 miles south of Augusta at the time.

"I'm not easily excitable, but this has left me with a strange weird feeling that I can't describe," she said.

The woman said she held a responsible job but would not identify herself. She said another woman was with her at the time and she, too, is extremely upset.

The woman said she was enroute from Louisville to Augusta when she spotted the light in a wooded section.

"At first we thought it was chain-lightning," she said. "I turned to my friend and asked her if she had seen it."

Then, she said, "out of the woods came this orange light." It rose above the tree tops and clearly outlined the trees. "We could even see the color of the trees."

Then the light moved along above the trees and parallel to the highway, keeping pace with the car. The light shown so brightly, she said, that a large area of the woods could be seen clearly.

She said it was difficult to estimate the size or the height of the object, or even how long it stayed in sight.

But, she added, the most upsetting part of the entire incident was the manner in which the object disappeared.

"It just weren't there anymore."

So, dear reader, continue to believe what you want. Continue to either accept or reject the accounts of so many UFO "eyewitnesses," including businessman Kenneth Arnold, textile mill employee Jack Reames, Augusta physician Colden Battey, numerous city policemen, county officers, highway patrolmen, military policemen, and, of course, President Jimmy Carter. If you could talk with them, no doubt they would tell you that they know what they saw—or maybe don't know what they saw, as the case may be.

But, either way, for more than half a century leading citizens of Georgia and the nation have wondered about the mysteries of unidentified flying objects and, most likely, will continue to wonder for countless years into the future.

CHAPTER 6

SAVANNAH'S WAVING GIRL

An amazing and history-making event happened in coastal Savannah, Georgia, on June 1, 1931: The "Waving Girl" stopped waving.

That last wave of her white handkerchief to a passing ship ended forty-four years of a world-famous tradition that lasted from 1887 until 1931. The never-married Florence Margaret Martus had waved her personal greetings to more than fifty thousand ships entering or leaving the mouth of the Savannah River where it opens into the Atlantic Ocean.

Why did she take on her solitary mission of waving to passing ships? There have been many explanations, including the most-repeated one: that Martus was hoping for a lover to return from overseas. But apparently nobody knows for sure. Martus herself denied the romantic theory and supposedly burned the diary she kept. She contended that she was simply waving hello to seafarers coming to the end of their journeys and waving good-bye to those starting new ones.

As she told one interviewer: "I was young, and it was sort of lonely on the island for a girl, so I started to wave to the ships which passed. They would return the greeting, and sometimes salute. Gradually they came to watch for my friendly wave from shore. We had many friends on the tugboats, and among the bar pilots."

To this day, though, the reason for her waving is a mystery. The millions of visitors who have gazed on the seven-foot statue of the Waving Girl, with a statue of her faithful collie by her side, have often wondered about that mystery.

And if you travel from the Waving Girl statue on Savannah's downtown riverfront fourteen miles east to Cockspur Island, you will find a Georgia Historical Commission marker erected in 1958 at Fort Pulaski near the visitor center parking lot. The inscription reads:

For 44 years, Florence Martus (1868–1943) lived on nearby Elba Island with her brother, the lighthouse keeper, and no ship arrived for Savannah or departed from 1887 to 1931 without her waving a handkerchief by day or a lantern by night. Throughout the years, the vessels in return watched for and saluted this quiet little woman. Few people ever met her yet she became the source of romantic legends when the story of her faithful greetings was told in ports all over the world. After her retirement the Propeller Club of Savannah, in honor of her seventieth birthday, sponsored a celebration on

Cockspur Island. A Liberty ship, built in Savannah in 1943, was named for her.

Florence's brother, George Washington Martus, was born in Washington, D.C., on May 31, 1861, at the start of the Civil War. In 1866 her father, Sergeant John H. Martus, moved her mother, Rosanna Cecelia Decker Martus, and their then four children to Cockspur Island when he was assigned to Fort Pulaski as an ordnance sergeant. The massive fort on Cockspur Island, where General Robert E. Lee had been stationed as a second lieutenant, was damaged by Union forces when they attacked and captured it early in the Civil War. Once the repairs to Fort Pulaski were finished, Sergeant Martus received a new assignment to be the keeper of the lighthouses on Cockspur and nearby Elba Island.

The lighthouse on Cockspur, built in 1848 two miles west of the Tybee Island lighthouse, became known as the South Channel Light. It helped guide ships heading up the Savannah River past Tybee, Cockspur, and Elba Islands.

On August 7, 1868, during Sergeant Martus's tour of duty at Fort Pulaski, his daughter Florence Margaret was born. The Martus family's life was interrupted in 1881 when a major hurricane destroyed their cottage near the fort. Later, when their father died and left them with the "family business" of taking care of the Cockspur and Elba lighthouses, George Martus and his sister Florence moved to a modest home on Elba Island. They also brought their widowed mother, whom they cared for until her death in 1909.

Before long, the lifesaving efforts of George and his sister Florence started to become legendary—not only in the Savannah area and other parts of Georgia but also around the nation and abroad. One such heroic effort took place in the wee hours of the morning when Florence spotted flames on the river and realized the U.S. government dredge that helped keep the Savannah River channel clear for boats was burning. She alerted her brother, and they leaped into their small boat and headed for the disaster. They were able to save more than thirty men, with the loss of only one crew member.

Over the years, thousands of letters from sailors around the world would find their way to Florence, to whom they faithfully acknowledged their dangerous way of life. Passengers wrote as well. One such passenger on board a New York–to–Savannah steamer recalled:

The first I saw of her was at sunrise. The little white cottage where she lived was close to the bank. She was a little thing, thin, but sturdy looking. The wind [was] whipping at her skirt and almost tore the cloth out of her hand. The sun showed her hair as gray and curly with red color still in it. Her eyes were blue. She wasn't pretty, but so alive. Her smile was one of the warmest I've ever seen. We saluted her with three blasts. I followed the ship's rail all the way to the stern, looking at her as long as she was visible.

Martus claimed that she waved at every vessel during her forty-four years on Elba Island. The famous war correspondent Ernie Pyle interviewed her and asked if she had ever missed a ship in all that time. She replied: "I was never too sick to get up when one was coming, and I could always hear them coming."

In 1923, the first of Chatham County's returning "dough-boys" from the allied troops' occupation of the Rhineland in Europe arrived back in Savannah to crowds cheering, bands playing, and the welcome greeting of their own hometown celebrity, the Waving Girl. A newspaper article described the scene:

> One of the features of the trip from Tybee [Island] bar into port will be the welcome of the Waving Girl, for many years known to seamen and to visitors who have made the trip in or out of Savannah harbor.
>
> Florence Martus is now nearly sixty years old, but she is still [known] to Savannah and the sailors [as] the "Waving Girl." From her home on the island mid-river, she has lived with her brother for several years since the death of her mother. Seventeen years ago [apparently a wrong figure], she began waving [at] every vessel that passed in or out of Savannah—with a white flag by day and a white lantern at night.
>
> Mariners have learned [of] her and sound their sirens as they approach—and even in the night she appears and waves her light, no matter how dark and stormy the night. There are many romantic stories as to the origin of

her customs—and all of them she either denies or smiles
at. Seamen from every port on earth however have in the
nearly two decades come to know her "wave" and consider it a good sign for them. It is declared that in seventeen years she has not failed to wave her flag or light for
any vessel that has sounded its whistle as it comes up the
river. She will be the first officially to greet the returning
American soldiers from the Rhine.

In December of that same year, a writer named M. Bishop
Alexander wrote from Liverpool, England, about seeing the
Waving Girl once again as he had many times before on his trips
to Savannah:

Thirteen minutes out of the slip at Savannah and bound
for Europe with a twenty-day stay on the big pond before
us, my newspaperman companion, Rob Parks, and I had
not a pang at leaving the states up to that time. Then we
passed the Waving Girl, and I am frank to confess there
was a moistness about my eyes that was suspiciously like
a tear and a lump in my throat I could not down.

Three salutatory blasts from the whistle of the *Sacan-
daga* and there appeared on the porch of a little white
frame cottage a slip of a woman with pearl gray hair;
in her hands a white cloth; perhaps her apron. Then
began the wave which has bade farewell and Godspeed
to thousands of sons of the sea, and it continued until

the modest home was lost from view as our ship steamed from the broadening mouth of the Savannah into the sparkling beckoning expanse of the Atlantic.

Carefully and quickly, I cast a glance about me. Rob, too, had been affected and on the bridge, Captain Jeffries, veteran master of ships, and his mates were pocketing handkerchiefs with which they had waved. Varied were the facial expressions; some were scowling sternly, others smiled as though relieved of some great burden and on the faces of still others could be read the appreciation of one of the sweetest sentiments of maritime history.

Alexander had a better grasp of how long Martus had been pursuing her love of waving to ships in reporting: "For thirty years or more, she has never been known to fail [to wave at ships] and her [white cloth] or the bright swinging lantern at night [have] grown to mean much to the men of the sea. To the accustomed or to the new initiated come the same thrill."

Over the years many people have wondered how Martus could have "heard" ships approaching on the river. The writer from Liverpool had his own theory: "Trained to set up a steady howling and yelping at the first sight of a ship, the dogs warn the Waving Girl and she is always ready with her greeting as a ship steams by. Day or night, no matter the weather or the hour, the Waving Girl of Savannah is there to greet a passing vessel."

After 1931, however, the Waving Girl would no longer be there to greet passing vessels. This long-standing tradition came to an end when her brother retired from the Lighthouse Service. She and her brother moved from their modest cottage on Elba Island to an apartment in Savannah at 642 East Liberty Street; later, she moved to the nearby town of Thunderbolt, a boating community on the Wilmington River. Newspapers everywhere bemoaned the retirement of the Waving Girl from her self-imposed mission in life.

The Augusta Chronicle published an editorial titled "The 'Waving Girl' Retires from Savannah Harbor." The editorial recounted stories about Martus that speculated as to why she began her waving and suggested—if she really did have a sailor sweetheart who never returned—that perhaps he was "ship-wrecked on some lonely island and became a Robinson Crusoe." The editorial reluctantly noted that there could be another possibility: that maybe her lover had found another sweetheart and decided to reject Martus. But the newspaper editorial writer did not want to believe that story and preferred to think that "even now in some land far away he is hoping for a reunion with his boyhood sweetheart."

At her retirement party, Martus was presented $500 (a large sum in 1931) from the maritime world and area citizens who appreciated her unique services. *The Augusta Chronicle* editorial further explained: "For she was popular, she was mysterious, and because of that mystery there was a glamour and romance about her life. . . . Let's think of romance in the life of the 'Waving Girl' and let not any plain, unvarnished and bare statement of facts other than the idyllic situation in our imagination come in to ruin the story."

When Martus's seventieth birthday rolled around on August 7, 1938, more than three thousand people gathered on the parade ground of historic Fort Pulaski to honor the Waving Girl. The celebration was sponsored by the Propeller Club. Martus was officially escorted from her home at Thunderbolt to Fort Pulaski, where the U.S. Marine Corps Band (most likely from Parris Island, South Carolina) and the Savannah Police Department Band entertained. The guests included many seafaring men who had looked forward to her waving them hello and good-bye. The parade ground was decorated with beautiful flags from ships and the flags of most nations. The Coast Guard cutter *Tallapoose* saluted Martus with its shrill whistle.

U.S. Congressman Hugh Peterson termed Martus "the sweetheart of mankind" and claimed that she was far better known in the ports of the world than any other Georgia citizen. This was an interesting boast, considering that one of Savannah's other famous citizens, who had died in 1927, was Juliette Gordon Low, founder of the Girl Scouts of the U.S.A. The congressman said that although Martus had chosen to live a rather lonely life on Elba Island, she had made herself a "benefactor to mankind by her wave of cheer."

Robert M. Hitch, Savannah's mayor, contended that the birthday celebration also was "in recognition of a sentiment that

This beautiful statue of the Waving Girl and her faithful collie continues to greet ships' crew and passengers on the Savannah River.

moved a bit of a young woman years ago to make a gesture of welcome to passing ships."

According to the program schedule, Martus was to deliver her own remarks, but she was overcome by the honors and presents and was unable to speak. She passed a handwritten note to the celebration's chairman, Edward A. Dutton, to read. It said simply, "This is the grandest day of my life."

Less than five years later, on February 8, 1943, Martus died in a Savannah hospital at the age of seventy-four. Her beloved brother, George, had died just a few years earlier on June 24, 1940. It is said that after Florence died, tugboats and other ships on the Savannah River lowered their flags to half-mast in deep respect.

The Waving Girl was buried beside her brother in Savannah's Laurel Grove Cemetery. The cemetery is also the final resting place of several members of Congress, more than six hundred Confederate soldiers, Girl Scouts of the U.S.A. founder Juliette Gordon Low, and James Pierpont, composer of the classic Christmas song "Jingle Bells."

In November 1943, nine months after her death, the SS *Florence Martus,* a Liberty ship, was launched as the thirteenth of eighty-eight Liberty ships built during World War II. It was one of the most fitting tributes to the woman who had waved to so many ships.

The memory of Florence Margaret Martus has only grown through the years since her death. In 1972 the people of

Savannah honored her and her faithful collie by erecting bronze statues, which were placed on a bluff off Savannah's downtown River Street. This riverside tribute was designed and created by sculptor Felix de Weldon, who also created the famous Marine Corps War Memorial showing five U.S. Marines raising the American flag at Iwo Jima. The statues of Martus and her collie were temporarily removed in September 1995 and put in storage during the construction of a river walk extension. Today, visitors once more can see Martus forever waving a cloth toward the river with her collie by her side. And they can visit the graves of Martus, her brother, and their parents in Laurel Grove Cemetery, near where I-16 flows into downtown Savannah.

And visitors continue to wonder, as have millions before them, about the mystery of Savannah's Waving Girl and why she waved to passing ships for forty-four years.

CHAPTER 7

GEORGE WASHINGTON'S FAVORITE NEPHEW

There was a solemn gathering in the graveyard of St. Paul's Episcopal Church in Augusta in mid-January 1809, as mourners watched the body of a thirty-seven-year-old man being lowered into his final resting place, a man whose life had been cut short by the same illness that had claimed his father. The man's passing was especially tragic because he left behind a wife and three sons in Virginia. His death may not have held great significance in the still-small town of Augusta had it not been for his connection to his famous uncle—George Washington, Revolutionary War hero and the first president of the United States.

And there were other significant and historic facts: His sister-in-law was future First Lady Dolley Madison, and when his widow remarried, her nuptials would be the first ever held in the White House.

Today, most visitors who wander the ancient gravestones of St. Paul's (on Reynolds Street at Sixth, just across from the Augusta Museum of History) are unaware of the significance of this grave. There is no marker, and his small, simple block headstone displays only his name, George Steptoe Washington, and the years of his birth and death. However, in 1809 St. Paul's was virtually the only place in Augusta where he could be buried with dignity. And he does rest forever near the remains of William Few, one of the two signers of the U.S. Constitution from Georgia; Robert Forsyth, the first U.S. federal law enforcement officer killed in the line of duty; and George Matthews, an early governor of Georgia.

But still the mystery lingers: Why is George Washington's nephew, considered by many historians to be his favorite, buried at St. Paul's rather than in his home state of Virginia? And what is the significance of his being buried next to a man named Ambrose Gordon?

"Respect This Stone," a small booklet printed by St. Paul's, gives an overview of the cemetery and offers this intriguing entry:

George Steptoe Washington (1774–January 10, 1809). There was no tombstone to mark the grave of George Steptoe Washington at the time of his death, but a marker was eventually placed there on October 5, 1956. However, an obituary in the *Augusta Herald* in January 1809 reads as follows: "Buried in St. Paul's Churchyard, George Steptoe Washington, Esquire, of Virginia, a nephew of the late President, in the 37th year of his age. His remains were yesterday deposited in St. Paul's Churchyard. Captain of the Eighth Virginia

Infantry, 1799. Honorably discharged June 10, 1800."
George Steptoe Washington, the fourth child of Colonel Samuel and Anne Steptoe Washington and nephew
of George Washington, was born at Harewood, the
Washington plantation, in Berkeley County, Virginia.
After having been educated in Virginia, he married
Lucy Payne of Philadelphia, sister of Dolley Payne
Todd Madison, in 1796. Captain Washington came
to Augusta for the purpose of recovering from poor
health, but he died ten days later, leaving a wife and
three children in Virginia.

If George Steptoe Washington did die in his thirty-seventh
year in January 1809, as the booklet states, then he would have
been born in 1771, not 1774. That is backed up by other sources
that claim he was born on August 17, 1771, at Harewood plantation in Jefferson County, Virginia.

As the booklet notes, his father was George Washington's brother, Samuel, who was born on November 16, 1734,
at Pope's Creek in Westmoreland County, Virginia—where
his brother, George, also was born. Samuel Washington held
numerous jobs in Stafford County, Virginia, including justice
of the peace, county magistrate, county sheriff, militia officer,
and parish vestryman. From 1735 to 1738 he lived at Mount
Vernon. He married five times and had seven children, including
George Steptoe Washington. In 1764 Samuel married his fourth
wife, Anne; his first three wives had died prematurely.

Washington family historian John Augustine Washington reports: "There's reason to believe she [Anne] brought a good deal of property with her, and I've always thought that it was partly with her resources that he began soon after this 1764 marriage to build the house at Harewood."

Samuel and Anne lived in Stafford County near Fredericksburg until 1770, the year before their son George's birth. Eventually Samuel would expand his Harewood plantation to 3,800 acres. That land, however, would be subdivided among children and grandchildren. The Harewood house, which still stands, now sits on 260 acres owned by Samuel Washington's descendants.

In 1781 Samuel died of tuberculosis. Harewood eventually passed on to George Steptoe Washington when he was just seventeen years of age. In 1793 Washington would marry fifteen-year-old Lucy Payne, the attractive younger sister of Dolley Payne Todd. Just a year after George and Lucy's marriage, her sister married James Madison (who in 1809 would become the fourth president of the United States) at Harewood. It was Dolley's second marriage. Her first husband, John Todd Jr., a lawyer, had died of yellow fever, leaving Dolley a widow with a young son.

As the nineteenth century dawned, tragedies continued to plague this wealthy and prominent family. Like his father, George Steptoe Washington had also contracted tuberculosis. He decided to head south to improve his health, leaving his young family behind in Virginia.

And, for some mysterious reason, he decided that the place he should go was Augusta, where his longtime friend, the late Ambrose Gordon, had lived. He also may have known that Augusta had warmly received his famous uncle during his 1791 presidential tour of the southern states and that it was Ambrose Gordon who had led the welcoming committee to officially greet the president as his party approached the town.

The journey south from Virginia to Georgia in a carriage on dirt roads must have been difficult for the tuberculosis-stricken George Steptoe Washington. He reached his destination shortly after Christmas 1808. But his stay in Augusta was not a joyful one. His condition deteriorated, and he died about ten days after arriving.

He had one last request, according to the booklet printed by St. Paul's: "Before his death . . . he had requested that he be buried near his dear friend, Colonel Ambrose Gordon." It is not totally clear how Gordon and Washington became such close friends, as Gordon was twenty years older than Washington. Perhaps Washington saw in Gordon some sort of father figure, since his own father had died when he was ten.

Who was the man whom George Washington's nephew regarded so highly that he wanted to spend eternity next to him? Ambrose Gordon was born in 1751 on his family's farm near Matchaponix, New Jersey. He had fought in the Revolution-ary War as a captain in a Virginia cavalry unit led by Lieuten-ant Colonel William Washington, a second cousin of George

DON RHODES

The grave markers of Ambrose Gordon (larger monument) and George Steptoe Washington (flat marker to the right) in the cemetery of St. Paul's Episcopal Church denote the final resting places of the two close friends.

Washington's. He settled in Augusta after the war and in 1787 married Betsey (Elizabeth) Mead. Gordon became a justice of the peace in Richmond County; a lieutenant colonel in the Richmond County Regiment, Georgia Militia; and Georgia's only U.S. marshal.

He and his wife had two sons and five daughters. In 1815 their oldest son, William Washington Gordon, became the first Georgian to graduate from the United States Military Academy at West Point, New York. He also became the first president of

Central of Georgia Railroad and Banking Company and mayor of Savannah. And even more significant, especially to millions of women, is the fact that one of Ambrose and Betsey Gordon's great-granddaughters was Juliette Gordon Low, founder of the Girl Scouts of the U.S.A.

Gordon died on June 28, 1804, at the age of fifty-three, and was buried in St. Paul's graveyard. Four years later, he would be reunited with his young Virginia friend. It will forever remain a mystery as to why George Washington's nephew wanted to spend his final days in Augusta and to be buried next to a much older friend, but visitors to the graveyard who know the connection cannot help but be touched by the eternal friendship of Ambrose Gordon and George Steptoe Washington.

CHAPTER 8

THE HOLLYWOOD STAR IN CARROLLTON

If you go to Carrollton, Georgia, forty miles west of Atlanta, then head north on US 27, then veer right onto GA 113 (also known as Temple Road), and take a left onto Old Centerpoint Road, you will come to Our Lady of Perpetual Help Catholic Church. Near the front of the church are the graves of former Carrollton businessman Eaton Chalkley, who died in January 1966 at the age of fifty-seven, and his wife, Susan, who died in March 1975, also at the age of fifty-seven. A large but simple marker over their graves says "F. Eaton Chalkley, 1909–1966" and "Mrs. F. E. Chalkley, 1917–1975," with the inscription "I am the resurrection and the life." That is all they wanted. But a few feet away is another marker placed by church officials, which is the one that many movie fans gaze upon with reverence. And it reads: "Grave of Susan Hayward Chalkley."

Susan Hayward—the same legendary actress who starred in such memorable films as *With a Song in My Heart, Back Street,*

I'd Climb the Highest Mountain, The President's Lady, Demetrius and the Gladiator, I'll Cry Tomorrow, Stolen Hours, The Snows of Kilimanjaro, I Can Get It for You Wholesale, and, of course, *I Want to Live,* for which she won the Oscar for Best Actress in 1959—is buried in this small, western Georgia Catholic cemetery. Right across the road from the church is the three-hundred-acre ranch that was the home of Susan and Eaton Chalkley for several years. Susan Hayward, a Brooklyn, New York, native, called this ranch "home," and it was here that she claimed to have spent the happiest time of her life. Moreover, it was Susan and Eaton Chalkley who donated the fourteen acres for the Our Lady of Perpetual Help church and who primarily financed the construction of the building itself.

Further confirmation of Hayward's love for this Georgia town is found in the Last Will and Testament she signed in Beverly Hills, California, on December 6, 1973. Item Fourteen in her will states, "I desire to be buried in Carrollton, Georgia. I shall leave funeral instructions with my sons or with others, as they need not be set forth in this will."

Susan Hayward was born in a Brooklyn apartment on June 30, 1917, as Edythe Marrenner. She had a career as a model, and that resulted in her being invited to Los Angeles for screen tests in December 1937 at the studios of David O. Selznick, executive producer of the Georgia-based epic *Gone with the Wind.* Her screen test was directed by George Cukor, who was fired as the director of *Gone with the Wind* three weeks after filming began.

In her biography *Susan Hayward: Portrait of a Survivor,* Beverly Linet quotes Cukor as denying the often-repeated story that Hayward was tested for the lead role of Scarlett O'Hara. However, Hayward did act as the stand-in for Miss Scarlett in the screen tests of other actors auditioning for the movie.

Oscar-winning star Susan Hayward loved her ranch life in rural North Georgia, far from the pressures of Hollywood.

Hayward was told that she didn't get a part in the movie and perhaps should consider going back to New York City. Nonetheless, she decided that a movie career was in her future and decided to stay. It was then that her name was changed from Edythe Marrenner to Susan Hayward. The last name was borrowed from that of Hollywood talent agent Leland Hayward, but no one seems to have remembered exactly where the first name Susan came from.

As her career took off, so did her love life, as many famous men became linked to her as suitors. She married the handsome actor Jess Barker (a native of Greenville, South Carolina) in a private ceremony in July 1944. No family members were present, and the only attendants were publicists Henry Rogers and Jean Pettebone. Her second marriage years later to Eaton Chalkley was done in the same ultra-private way. Barker and Hayward divorced in 1954; their union had produced twin sons, Timothy and Gregory.

In early 1950 an interesting chain of events led Hayward to take up permanent residence in Georgia. It began with actress Jeanne Crain's becoming pregnant by her husband, Paul Brinkman, and having to drop out of filming on the movie *I'd Climb the Highest Mountain*. Crain had been cast to portray a Methodist circuit preacher's wife in rural north Georgia opposite actor William Lundigan. Darryl F. Zanuck, head of the Twentieth Century Fox film company, replaced Crain with Hayward. As a result of her participation in the project, Hayward became immersed in Georgia culture. The film was based on the autographical book *The Circuit Rider's Wife* by Georgia native Corra Harris, and it was produced by Atlanta native Lamar Trotti, said to be the first graduate of the University of Georgia's Henry W. Grady School of Journalism.

The main filming locations for *I'd Climb the Highest Mountain* were around Dawsonville and Cleveland in White and Habersham Counties in north-central Georgia. Hayward apparently fell in love not only with Georgia but also with many of its people, most notably a heavy-set, highly likable guy named Harvey Hester. He co-owned and ran Aunt Fanny's Cabin, a popular restaurant in Smyrna, north of Atlanta, where the film's cast and crew liked to eat. In the process, Hayward came to know and like Hester, who was cast in a bit part in the movie.

Aunt Fanny's Cabin had humble beginnings. In 1941 Isoline Campbell MacKenna converted an 1890s-era cabin on her property to a country store that sold preserves and vegetables grown on her farm. MacKenna also sold food prepared from the recipes of Fanny Williams, the MacKenna family's retired cook. Eventually the store evolved into a restaurant called Aunt Fanny's Cabin.

Harvey Hester and Marjorie Bowman bought the restaurant in 1946 and operated it for twenty-two years. It became one of "the" places to be seen in Atlanta, with scores of celebrities finding their way to its great southern cooking. In 1968 the restaurant was taken over by George Poole; Frank Johnson bought Aunt Fanny's Cabin in 1992 but closed it in 1994.

You can still visit the same rooms where Susan Hayward used to eat with Harvey Hester. The two former Aunt Fanny's Cabin buildings (the original 1890s cabin and its added-on 1940s terrace room) were moved from their original location on Campbell Road to 2875 Atlanta Rd. They now are used as the Smyrna Welcome Center, located next to the Smyrna Museum. The six-acre property where Aunt Fanny's Cabin was located is now the site of a luxury-homes subdivision.

In December 1955 Hayward attended a cocktail party thrown by Vincent Flaherty, columnist for the *Los Angeles Examiner* newspaper. Her date was none other than Aunt Fanny's co-owner, Harvey Hester, who also knew Flaherty. Hester was there to meet a new fellow Georgian named Eaton Floyd Chalkley Jr., who recently had moved to Carrollton. Chalkley, previously married with three children, had been an FBI agent and a lawyer for General Motors. He had discovered the peaceful town of Carrollton during a trip to Atlanta. He ended up buying a farm outside town as well as the local General Motors dealership, which sold Chevrolets, Cadillacs, and Oldsmobiles. Chalkley was a childhood friend of Flaherty's, and Flaherty thought his friend would get better settled in the Atlanta area if he met Hester, who knew just about everybody worth knowing.

Hayward and Chalkley met at the party and began their courtship. Eventually, the two slipped off to Phoenix, Arizona, and were married there on February 9, 1957, by a justice of the peace. He was forty-eight, and she was thirty-nine. There was neither a matron of honor nor a best man, although Flaherty had been invited to do the honors. The couple's decision to get married was so sudden that Flaherty wasn't able to join them in Phoenix. After a honeymoon in New Orleans, the couple began their married life on Chalkley's ranch outside Carrollton. Hayward immediately began exchanging her former life as an international movie star for that of a down-home country girl. She canned fruits and vegetables, rode into town in a pickup truck, shopped in local stores where the clerks and owners called her Mrs. Chalkley, and, in general, was just one of the local folks. However, she did not completely abandon her film career.

In 1958 the Chalkleys formed a corporation for moviemaking, building and operating motels and restaurants, and conducting a loan and insurance business.

Chalkley apparently adjusted to his new status as the husband of a movie star. A *New York Daily News* reporter once asked him if he felt that he was playing a minor role being married to a celebrity. He reportedly replied, "How can a fellow ever feel he's playing a minor role when he's playing the role for real of Susan's husband? I love to stand around and watch people rave over her." On the occasions when Chalkley did visit Hayward on movie sets, he stayed in the background behind the cameras and did not offer any filming advice. He confidently and self-assuredly knew that once the cameras stopped rolling, Mrs. Chalkley would be heading back to Georgia with him and their lives would return to normal.

Just a few months before Chalkley and Hayward met, a grim incident appeared in the news. On June 3, 1955, a former prostitute and drug addict named Barbara Graham was executed in the gas chamber of San Quentin prison in California. Graham had been convicted of the 1953 beating death of Mable Monohan, an elderly widow who lived in the Burbank suburb of Los Angeles. Graham and some cohorts were under the wrong impression that Monohan had lots of jewels in her house. Three years after Graham's execution, Hayward began filming a story based on Graham's life that raised doubts as to her guilt. That movie, *I Want to Live*, earned Hayward her only Oscar for Best Actress.

The Academy Awards ceremony was held in Los Angeles on Monday night, April 6, 1959. The following Thursday, Hayward and her husband flew back to their home in Georgia. They were met at the Atlanta airport by a large delegation headed by Carrollton Mayor Stewart Martin. They then embarked on a motorcade that stretched for more than two miles, with thousands of well-wishers lining the route into Carrollton. In a brief ceremony at Chalkley's automobile dealership, the mayor presented Hayward with a key to the city. Asked if she had any hunch that she might win while sitting in the Academy Awards audience, Hayward replied, "I'm not a mind reader. . . . I just hoped."

Life continued to be good for the Chalkleys, who bought a ranch of roughly six hundred acres near Heflin, Alabama, just across the state line. They named it Chalkmar, a combination of "Chalkley" and "Marrenner" (Hayward's real name). They turned the ranch into a productive cattle-breeding company that eventually boasted more than two hundred cows. In addition they kept horses, which the Chalkleys rode along with Hayward's twin sons, who had been attending Georgia Military Academy in Milledgeville.

About this time, Chalkley apparently had become weary of driving to a Catholic church in Cedartown, Georgia, thirty-one miles away, whenever he wanted to attend weekday services. So he approached the diocese about donating fourteen acres of land for a new Our Lady of Perpetual Help Catholic Church, which had been holding services only on weekends in a small, old building. Chalkley also offered to finance the construction of the new church. He talked the diocese into moving the center of the parish from Cedartown to the new church building in Carrollton.

Tragedy struck the Chalkley family in September 1964 when Joe Chalkley, Eaton's son from his first marriage, died at the age of twenty-six. He was killed when a plane he was piloting crashed into a mountainside near Louisville, Kentucky, during a thunderstorm. Chalkley apparently never recovered from his son's death. Two years later, on January 9, 1966, Chalkey died of liver disease in Fort Lauderdale, Florida, where Eaton and Susan had a vacation home. Hayward received permission to bury her husband near the entrance of Our Lady of Perpetual Help. That, in turn, was the beginning of the cemetery at the church that meant so much to both of them. She supervised the landscaping for the cemetery and the design of the monument over her husband's grave. His death, however, was so traumatic for Hayward that she rarely returned to their Carrollton ranch; instead, she divided her time between her homes in Fort Lauderdale and Beverly Hills.

She attempted to resume her show-business career, making her final feature film, *Valley of the Dolls,* in early 1967. She played aging movie star Helen Lawson, a role that was originally assigned to Judy Garland. The movie is especially memorable for a scene in which a younger movie star (portrayed by Patty Duke) gets in a fight with Hayward's character and rips her wig off.

In 1972 Hayward was diagnosed with inoperable brain cancer. Still, that year she completed filming for two made-for-television movies, *The Revengers* and *Say Goodbye Maggie Cole*. Her last public appearance was at the 1974 Oscars ceremony, where she joined Charlton Heston to present the Best Actress Award to Ellen Burstyn for portraying a strong single mother in *Alice Doesn't Live Here Anymore*. Heston had costarred with Hayward in the 1953 movie *The President's Lady*. In July 1974 the Associated Press reported that Hayward had been admitted to Emory Hospital in Atlanta and was in "good condition." The article said that a brain biopsy had been performed by her physician, George Tindall, and that the hospital had been "flooded with phone calls [and] well wishers attempting to deliver flowers and fruit to the actress." The hospital refused to accept the flowers and gifts "because there is no place to put them," according to a spokesman.

Less than eight months later, Hayward died in her Beverly Hills home. Her body was flown to Atlanta and then driven to Almon Funeral Home in Carrollton. One of Hayward's doctors, Lee Siegel, told the media that Hayward's case was amazing because most people with her multiple malignant brain tumors lived only six weeks to three months after diagnosis. He added, "But she had a tremendous desire to live. She was a terrific fighter."

Hayward's funeral was held on March 16, 1975, a rainy, cold Sunday, in Our Lady of Perpetual Help Catholic Church.

Her casket was covered with yellow roses and white orchids. Her twin sons, Timothy and Gregory Barker, were among the pall-bearers. More than five hundred mourners packed the church. The Requiem Mass was celebrated by three priests and Monsignor Michael Regan, who had become pastor of the church in 1972. Regan called the Chalkleys "great, great benefactors" of the church, adding, "The evidence which they gave of their love of our holy faith will continue to be green in this beautiful and peaceful area for many years to come, praise God."

And on that rainy March day in north Georgia, Oscar-winning actress Susan Hayward was laid to eternal rest beside her beloved husband.

CHAPTER 9

WHO BUILT ROCK EAGLE AND THE MOUNDS?

Georgia is full of many mysteries related to the thousands of Native Americans who inhabited the area long before it became a British colony or a state.

One of those mysteries concerns a large, man-made formation of milky-white quartz rocks off GA 441 about nine miles north of Eatonton, just south of I-20. The formation is so large that when you stand next to it, you see only a pile of rocks. But when you climb the nearby three-story tower and gaze upon the same area, you see an amazing resemblance to a giant bird, which is why this formation is known as Rock Eagle. At the tallest point of its breast, the height is 10 feet. The main body of the bird is 35 feet wide and 102 feet from head to tail, with a wingspan of 120 feet. It is regarded as the largest stone effigy in the United States.

What is its meaning? Why was it constructed? No one knows for sure, but most interpretations agree that it was made by Native Americans (most likely Woodland Indians or Lower

The mystery remains regarding who originally built this formation of rocks in the shape of a giant eagle not far from Eatonton, Georgia.

Creeks) who used it for religious purposes and other ceremonial activities. Estimates of its age vary from two thousand to five thousand years old. The site on which the Rock Eagle is located comprises the largest 4-H center in Georgia (http://rockeagle4h .org), with 1,428 acres of forestlands and a 110-acre lake. The University of Georgia's College of Agricultural and Environmental Sciences Cooperative Extension provides 4-H programs at Rock Eagle, including summer camping experiences and environmental education programs.

Charles Colcock Jones Jr., a Georgia historian and former mayor of Savannah, is credited with making the first measurements of Rock Eagle in 1877. He long had an interest in Native Americans, which culminated in his international classic *Antiquities of the Southern Indians, Particularly of the Georgia Tribes* (1873). A. R. Kelly of the University of Georgia excavated the site in 1935, and another excavation was done in 1954. Neither dig turned up any significant artifacts. The site became a 4-H center in 1955 and in 1978 was added to the U.S. Department of Interior's National Register of Historic Places. In 1990 the Georgia Department of Resources joined with the Putnam County Board of Commissioners, the University of Georgia, the Georgia Power Company, and the Oconee Regional Planning and Development office to preserve the unusual formation, which draws thousands of visitors each year. The eagle itself is somewhat protected by a chain link fence.

Just fifteen miles away in Putnam County is another stone effigy. This formation, which has a tail resembling that of a hawk, is known as Rock Hawk. It is located adjacent to Lawrence Shoals Recreation Park along GA 16. It measures 102 feet from head to tail, but its main body is 75 feet wide, more than double that of Rock Eagle. Rock Hawk measures 132 feet from wing tip to wing tip, slightly longer than Rock Eagle's wingspan.

Almost as mysterious as Rock Eagle and Rock Hawk are various burial and ceremonial mounds, which are attributed to early Native Americans. They are scattered throughout Georgia, with the best known being the Etowah Mounds, the Kolomoki Mounds, and the Ocmulgee Mounds.

Etowah Mounds: Located on the banks of the Etowah River in northeast Georgia near Cartersville, five miles southwest of I-75, exit 288. This fifty-four-acre state park, containing six earthen mounds believed to date from A.D. 1000 to 1550, is regarded as the most intact Mississippian Culture site in the southeastern United States.

The largest of the mounds is a sixty-three-foot flat-topped knoll, which possibly served as the home of the priest-chief. Excavations of the site uncovered a mound in which Indian nobility were believed to be buried in elaborate costumes with items for their afterlives, much like ancient Egyptian burial customs. The interpretative center on the site displays objects created of wood, seashells, and stone, including clay figurines found in the vicinity.

There also is a nature trail leading to the Etowah River. Experts say that the complex, which includes a moat and a fortification system, resembles the creations of Muskogean-speaking Creeks. The Etowah Mounds became a registered National Historic Site in 1964.

Kolomoki Mounds: Located in southwest Georgia on a tributary of the Chattahoochee River, six miles north of Blakely off US 27. This state park features Georgia's oldest great temple mound, four ceremonial mounds, and two burial mounds. It is believed to have been one of the most populous settlements of early Native Americans north of Mexico.

The highest of the seven mounds is fifty-six feet. Two of the mounds are believed to have been burial repositories. Excavations have turned up ceramic vessels decorated in animal and human forms. Archaeologist William Sears, who researched the site in the late 1940s and early 1950s, believed that the site dated to the Mississippian Period (A.D. 800–1600), but other archaeologists now recognize that Kolomoki was occupied mainly in the Woodland Period (1000 B.C.–A.D. 900).

In March 1974 thieves broke into the museum of Kolomoki Mounds State Historic Park and stole 129 artifacts. Reportedly, some of the items have been recovered from collectors and flea markets in Florida and Pennsylvania, but the whereabouts of the bulk of them remain a mystery.

Ocmulgee Mounds: Located on the banks of the Ocmulgee River in middle Georgia on the eastern fringe of Macon, off I-16, exit 2, on Emery Highway (US 80). Apparently, the river was a great source of exploration and discovery for the ancient tribes who inherited this area. Here the Ocmulgee River flows into the Altamaha River, which flows into the Atlantic Ocean.

These mounds were noted in reports by a Georgia Guard member under the command of Georgia founder and British General James Oglethorpe and by the noted naturalist William Bartram in the 1770s. The site consists of a large temple mound that rises some forty-five feet high and offers a great view of the Ocmulgee River; a smaller temple mound; and other formations believed to have been constructed around A.D. 900–950 during the Early Mississippian Period.

As a result of archaeologist A. R. Kelly's findings, the Ocmulgee National Park was created in 1936. In *The New Georgia Encyclopedia,* Mark Williams of the University of Georgia reports that the Ocmulgee site was abandoned by about A.D. 1100. The fate of its inhabitants are still a mystery.

Besides these three locations, a number of excavations of former Native American sites have been conducted throughout Georgia over the years. One of the richest finds was on Stallings Island in the Savannah River, north of Augusta. In March 1929 *The Chronicle* reported that excavations had been under way on

Stallings Island thanks to the interest of William H. Claflin Sr. of Boston, who had been spending his winters in Augusta. The newspaper said that Claflin had financed the excavations for the Peabody Museum of Harvard University, which sent archaeologist C. B. Cosgrove to direct the research work.

"Although handicapped in their work by rains," the newspaper reported, "their discovery warrants their belief that these inhabitants, whose 72 graves were opened, were pre-historic tribes living probably five to six hundred years ago, and there is little evidence to show that they had ever had contact with the whites except in the instance of one small find—two bits of glass—which could have served as Spanish or colonial trade pieces." The article also noted, "One of the important things discovered was the manner of burying the dead. Unlike the customs [of] many tribes of Indians, few offerings were interred with the bodies, only several shell beads being found. . . . One very interesting find was the skeleton of an infant that had been interred in a kind of urn or jar."

About a decade later, more artifacts were discovered on Stallings Island by a Works Progress Administration crew led by Paul M. Myers under the sponsorship of the University of Georgia and the Georgia Department of Natural Resources. In April 1940 *The Chronicle* wrote about these findings: While searching in a mound on the island, Myers's crew had found pottery with reed markings "entirely different from the pottery found anywhere else by archaeologists." Additionally, the skeletons of a man and a woman were found, along with house posts and refuse pits.

"At present the mound is about 450 feet long and 15 feet high," *The Chronicle* reported. "The top is covered with sea shells to a depth of about four feet. The shells must have been carried up the river from the coast by Indians, Mr. Myers observed."

Besides the mysteries associated with Rock Eagle and Rock Hawk and a number of mounds constructed by Native Americans, there is an even deeper and possibly older mystery: Who built the great stone wall that stretches more than 850 feet along the highest area of Fort Mountain in northeast Georgia and that in places reaches as high as seven feet?

According to archaeologists, the fortification long predates the Cherokees, who lived in northeast Georgia in the 1700s. A Cherokee legend says that the wall was created by moon-eyed people with blonde hair and blue eyes. Some researchers and historians believe the wall has a religious or ceremonial purpose since the sun illuminates the wall at both sunrise and sunset. Still others believe the wall was constructed by Woodlands Indians between 500 B.C. and A.D. 500. It appears similar to walls that existed around the top of Stone Mountain near Atlanta and possibly around both Rock Eagle and Rock Hawk. Some outlandish stories even claim the wall is tied to Prince Madoc, an explorer from Wales who supposedly landed on the shores of Mobile Bay, Alabama, in 1170 and left area Native Americans speaking Welsh.

Jared Wood, manager of the archaeology lab at the University of Georgia, doesn't buy that theory. He said, "There has been no archaeological evidence to back up stories that either this Welsh prince or any others came to explore the New World. We're not exactly sure what purposes these [fortlike] enclosures served, but they were likely well-known gathering places for social events." He added, "Seasonal meetings of friends and kin, trading of goods, astronomical observance, and religious or ceremonial activities may have occurred there."

In 1810 John Sevier, the first governor of Tennessee, in a letter to someone researching the history of Louisiana, addressed the possibility of Welsh explorers in the pre-Columbian New World. The governor wrote that in 1782, when he was on a campaign against the Cherokees, he talked at length with "a venerable old chief called Oconostota" and asked the chief what he knew of any pre-Columbian explorer sites in the Southeast. In response, the chief said that his forefathers had told of fortifications in north Georgia that had been made by white people called Welsh. The governor added, "Many years ago I happened in company with a French-man, who had lived with the Cherokees and said he had formerly been high up the Missouri. He informed me he had traded with the Welsh tribe; that they certainly spoke much of the Welsh dialect, and tho' their customs were savage and wild yet many of them, particularly the females, were very fair and white, and frequently told him that they had sprung from a white nation of people."

Many mysteries relating to the Native Americans of Georgia will continue to pass down through the ages, for no one ever will know the true meanings of the giant bird effigies, the ceremonial mounds, or the great and mysterious wall in the north Georgia mountains.

CHAPTER 10

AMERICA'S FIRST WONDER WOMAN

In the Victorian era, the prevailing images of women were stay-at-home mothers who were weak, helpless creatures. Men were supposed to be their family's breadwinners and a strong protector who engaged in manly, muscular activities.

Then, in the late 1800s, along came a buxom teenager from a small Georgia town who could throw men around a stage and exceed them in other public exhibitions of physical strength. Instead of being outraged, the men and women of America loved her and packed the largest theaters across the nation to see this amazing young woman, who was billed as "the Georgia Wonder."

Lula Hurst (commonly called Lulu in media about her life) was born in 1869 in rural Polk County, Georgia, near the Alabama state line. Her childhood years apparently were as normal as any other girl until the night of September 18, 1883, following a severe electrical storm.

Reportedly, the fourteen-year-old Lula and her family heard unexplained quick, muffled, popping sounds. After that

Lula suddenly had miraculous physical powers. She was able to move objects at will and could cause rapping sounds on tables in response to her questions: one rap for "yes" and two raps for "no." Neighbors who began hearing of her remarkable new powers flocked to the Hurst farmhouse. There they found that the teenager could also drag strong men holding walking canes, umbrellas, or billiard cue sticks, despite the fact that she weighed only about 120 pounds and stood five feet six-and-a-half inches tall.

Within months, she had attracted the attention of Paul Atkinson of Madison, Georgia (halfway between Atlanta and Augusta), who became her manager and husband. Henry W. Grady, the famous publisher and editor of *The Atlanta Constitution*, also became fascinated by her. Grady assigned his top reporter, Josiah Carter, to cover her exploits. And just like wildfire, the news about the young woman dubbed "the Georgia Wonder" began to spread rapidly across the nation.

In 1884, during her first full year of performing, she became the toast of New York City with a series of shows at Wallack's Theater in Manhattan. The *New York Times*, however, was less than impressed, pointing out that her adoring fans did not seem to care if her "powers" were actually due to her ability to place men in physical positions where they were off balance or where they could be influenced by mental suggestions. In fact, on July 12 the *Times* stated that her stage act "only proves the philosopher who said that the public likes to be fooled."

Nevertheless, the newspaper conceded that the Georgia Wonder was a powerful force to behold as far as her stage charisma and abilities to charm an audience:

> Galleries, balconies, orchestra chairs, boxes and aisles were crowded, and the rest of the populace were jammed at the doors and climbing up each other's backs in frantic efforts to catch a glimpse of the stage. It was an audience for the most part that came to be amused and cared not how that object was accomplished or even if they helped to afford the amusement themselves, but some of them were Pickwickian scientists who were going to sift the mysterious force that enables a girl to break an umbrella or shove a man burdened with a heavy chair about a stage before a wondering world.

The *Times* related that the host of Hurst's show, her personal manager Paul Atkinson, requested that twelve gentlemen come up to the stage to participate in her exhibitions of physical prowess. However, one of those "gentlemen" was Professor D. L. Dowd, one of the first well-known bodybuilders in America who would author a best-selling book on physical culture.

"Dowd has a record for lifting 1,442 pounds from the floor with his hands, and he gave exhibitions of strength with the Barnum circus in Madison Square Garden last spring," the newspaper reported. "He took his seat quietly with the others and awaited developments." But Dowd made his presence known after Hurst "over-powered" one of the twelve gentlemen who had tried to hold onto a walking cane when she put her hand over his.

"Dowd, who had been watching the girl's experiments, now asked to be allowed to take the cane. The girl put her hands against it and pushed, but Dowd pushed the harder, and with very little exertion shoved her back against the scene, while the spectators shouted and screamed and hooted. 'It's only muscular force,' said Dowd as he sat down. 'She puts her hand against the cane and pushes, that's all.'" As the performance progressed, the packed crowd, not happy with what Dowd was doing in over-coming the star of the show, began to see him as a spoiler.

"Miss Hurst next did the billiard cue trick, and a light-waisted boy was unable to put the end to the floor because she had her arm under it and pressed upward with the palm of her hand, thus getting a tremendous purchase," the newspaper reported. "Dowd, however, in spite of her advantage put the end of the cue on the floor with scarcely an effort and again there was a pandemonium of cheers and hisses."

At one point, when Dowd asked to be permitted to come up once again and try to do something that others had failed to do, Paul Atkinson smiled "but refused him gently and firmly." It was obvious that the personal manager did not like Dowd upstaging his moneymaker. "All the wonder here is the woman's strength," Dowd said after Hurst prevented a "wild-eyed young man" from forcing down a chair he was holding. "It is only muscular effort applied strategically. She had studied this and takes advantage of everything."

The *Times*'s detailed article supposedly revealed Hurst as being somewhat like a magician whose tricks had been exposed. Nonetheless, five days later, on July 17, 1884, the newspaper reported on the Georgia Wonder's matinee performance at Wallack's Theater for a full house filled only with women. All men had been banished from the theater, except for Atkinson, the show's host. "The umbrella trick was done with great success and a bonnet was wrecked in the experiment," the *Times* reported. "The cane and billiard cue acts also went off with as much zest as the masculine audiences do in the evening, and, Manager Frank Bixby, who stood upon the outside steps of the theatre with the doors locked and the key in his pocket, said he had not heard so much cackling before since his grandparents were children."

Amazingly, just as quickly as Hurst's show-business career had taken off, it ended, after only two years of performances. For whatever reasons, she decided that she had had enough of touring and being challenged by disbelievers who knew what she actually did: that her physical powers were really the result of mind over matter as well as balance. She herself would reveal those powers in her autobiography, published in 1897. Hurst married her personal manager, Paul Atkinson, and they lived a quiet life in a glorious, two-story house at 433 South Main St. in Madison, Georgia. They named their first-born child, Grady, after her loyal supporter Henry W. Grady, who had died days before their son's birth. After his wife's retirement from the stage, Atkinson continued to dabble in show business of sorts.

In 1883, the same year that Hurst discovered her amazing "powers," the American Panorama Company in Madison, Wisconsin, was commissioned to create two enormous cyclorama paintings depicting the Civil War battles of Atlanta and Missionary Ridge. In 1887 the company's manager, William Wehner, first displayed the battle of Atlanta painting in Detroit, Michigan. The next year, however, Wehner ran into financial difficulties and passed ownership of the painting to the heirs of a family who owned the land where the painting was housed.

The family in turn sold the painting in 1890 to Paul Atkinson, who had already bought the companion Missionary Ridge cyclorama painting. Atkinson put the Missionary Ridge painting on display in a round building on Edgewood Avenue in Atlanta until 1892, when he loaned it for display in Nashville, Tennessee. Unfortunately, the painting was destroyed in a tornado.

In 1892 Atkinson replaced the Missionary Ridge painting in the Edgewood Avenue building with the battle of Atlanta painting. The next year, he sold the painting to a man from Florida. Today the painting is world famous and is displayed in the Cyclorama building at Grant Park in Atlanta.

As famous as she was at the turn of the twentieth century, many of Lula Hurst Atkinson's relatives are just now learning about her stage days.

*Graves of Lula (or sometimes Lulu) Hurst Atkinson and her husband
Paul Atkinson in the Madison city cemetery.*

Tom Atkinson, her great-great nephew and a minister in
Union City, Tennessee, explains that though she was commonly
referred to as Lulu, her true name was Lula. "I think the Lulu
thing came from people getting the name mixed up, and she
used it herself at times. However, I've seen the only remaining
panel from her foot locker that she carried on her trips, and it is
stamped 'Lula' instead of 'Lulu.'"

Tom recently self-published a family history that contains close
to two hundred pages of stories and three hundred pages of photos.
He edited and compiled the book with his cousin, Carol Atkinson
Cross, of Madison, who was especially helpful in his research.

Robert Thompson Atkinson of Young Harris, Georgia, also spoke of his grandmother, saying:

It is sad that I know so little about my grandmother, Lula. I did not know of her stage career until a number of years after she died. Nothing was printed about her that I saw until the late '50s when the series of articles in the *Atlanta Journal* about famous Georgia women came out. My father Grady (her second son) was so protective of her identity.

Even after her death, it [her stage life] was never even spoken of in our home. As a boy growing up, she was just a kindly grandmother who could whip up marvelous angel food cakes. There are no surviving snapshots of the time from early 1900s and very few formal pictures. She and my grandfather [Paul] bought the house soon after their marriage when they came to live in Madison.

Apparently they entertained locally but mostly literary events because of Paul's interest in Chatauga events. They provided a home for Lula's sister's two children when they were orphaned, a brother's children during Depression days, as well as another young girl relative who needed a home. After his death in the early 1930s, Lula had a difficult time financially. She ran a boarding house for local teachers, and, when her first son, Paul, became ill with stomach cancer, she nursed him until his death.

One of those children that Lula raised was Margaret Nix Ponder of Atlanta, who especially remembers Mrs. Atkinson as a very loving woman. Mrs. Ponder recalled, "I was two years old when I went to live with the Atkinsons. I grew up in their house in Madison until I left to go to Agnes Scott College. She was quite an unusual person, but her stage life was never mentioned in our family. Never. I think she had hated it."

Ponder's daughter, Paullin Judin, also observed:

Unlike most women of that age, Lula Atkinson attended Shorter College in Rome, Georgia. She and Paul also taught elocution classes and competed in district meets. They had two sons of their own, Grady and Paul D., and they also helped raise five other children. They provided for Emmet Craddock, Evelyn Hurst Lilly, Maude Peek, and Alma Craddock Furlow during their high school and college years. They took my mother, Margaret (Denaro) Nix, in at age two and raised her. During the Depression, they also provided room and board for some of the teachers, and they fixed lunches every day for four boys from Rutledge, Georgia, and another teacher who came to Madison for their tenth and eleventh grades of high school. Then during World War II, while my father was away, they took Mother and my two oldest sisters in to live with them.

So Lula Atkinson was [known] for her great power, but she was also a very kind, generous, and loving person who accepted several young people into her home in Madison during those days. Mother noted that she was so well liked by the young people and that boys would often stop and talk with her if she was out sitting on her porch. Mother was very proud to have had "Louie" as her guardian.

Paul Atkinson died in 1931 at the age of seventy-three. His once-famous wife survived him by nineteen years, dying on May 13, 1950. The Wonder Woman and the Cyclorama Man now rest forever in the Madison city cemetery.

On her gravestone, ordered and placed by her son, Grady, are these simple words:

LULA HURST

WIFE OF

PAUL M. ATKINSON

1869–1950

In death, she was not to be known as "The Georgia Wonder" but simply as a good mother and kind grandmother who could whip up some marvelous angel food cakes.

CHAPTER 11

WHERE IS BUTTON GWINNETT?

In the late 1700s duels were not uncommon in Georgia. So it was not a strange sight to see the two men meeting on the outskirts of Savannah—in an area thought to be present-day Thunderbolt, Georgia, on the western shore of the Wilmington River—for a duel with pistols to "resolve" a matter of honor, which usually involved either a woman or a damaged reputation.

On this particular warm day of May 16, 1777, the two duelists, along with their seconds (basically assistants), were resolving a dispute over what one man felt was a damaged reputation. Both were shot with fairly well-placed bullets, but only one of those wounds would prove fatal, after gangrene infected the man's shattered leg, causing his death three days later.

It also was not unusual that this duel involved two extremely well-known figures—such was often the case in the colonial South, where tempers were heightened by the American Revolution and its intense political maneuverings. However,

Although this elaborate monument in Savannah's Colonial Park Cemetery honors Button Gwinnett, most experts believe the Declaration of Independence signer is buried elsewhere.

given that the loser of that duel was none other than Button Gwinnett, who had signed the Declaration of Independence less than a year earlier, it is very strange—and a great mystery—that no one knows exactly where he is buried. Some say he was buried in Colonial Park Cemetery, where his dueling partner, Lachlan McIntosh, is interred. Others believe that he was buried on St. Catherine's Island (south of Savannah off the Georgia coast), which he owned.

Colonial Park Cemetery contains an imposing monument accompanied by a plaque that honors Gwinnett. The plaque reads:

THIS MEMORIAL TO

BUTTON GWINNETT

BORN 1735 DIED 1777

GEORGIA SIGNER OF THE DECLARATION OF INDEPENDENCE

PRESIDENT OF GEORGIA

WHOSE REMAINS, BURIED IN THIS CEMETERY, ARE BELIEVED TO

LIE ENTOMBED HEREUNDER.

WAS ERECTED BY THE

SAVANNAH—CHATHAM COUNTY

HISTORIC SITE AND MONUMENT COMMISSION

WITH MONIES CONTRIBUTED BY

THE STATE OF GEORGIA—THE CITY OF SAVANNAH

AND THE GEORGIA SOCIETIES OF THE

SONS OF THE REVOLUTION, DAUGHTERS OF

THE AMERICAN REVOLUTION

SOCIETY OF COLONIAL WARS AND
COLONIAL DAMES OF AMERICA
ERECTED 1964 BY SAVANNAH—CHATHAM COUNTY
HISTORIC SITE AND MONUMENT COMMISSION

Although the plaque says this is the spot where Gwinnett's remains "are believed to lie entombed," more recent research calls that notion into question. Zell Miller, former U.S. senator and Georgia governor, writes in his book *Great Georgians* (1983):

> Even today there is considerable dispute as to whether the bones buried in the grave marked as his in Colonial Cemetery in Savannah are actually his. Some believe he was buried atop an Indian mound near his home on St. Catherine's Island and that his bones were washed out to sea during a hurricane. Residents of that area say two ghosts of Gwinnett haunt that barrier island, one on his horse returning from Philadelphia and the other at the helm of his boat, *Beggar's Benison.*

Meanwhile, at the Gwinnett County Courthouse in Lawrenceville, Georgia, near Atlanta, an informative Georgia Historical Commission marker states:

> Button Gwinnett, for whom this county was named, was born in Gloucestershire, England, in 1735, the son of a Church of England minister. He worked in the

store of his father-in-law in Dexter for two years, then as an importer and exporter for three years. In 1765 he came to Georgia, opening a store in Savannah. The same year he sold his store, bought St. Catherine's Island and moved onto it, becoming a familiar figure at Sunbury and Midway Church.

Button Gwinnett was elected Justice of the Peace in 1767; Commissioner of Pilotage in 1768; member of the Georgia Assembly (legislature) in 1769. He was sent to the Continental Congress early in 1776 and signed the Declaration of Independence Aug. 2, 1776. He later served as Speaker of the Assembly and was one of the chief drafters of the first State Constitution.

Mr. Gwinnett was chosen to fill the unexpired term of Archibald Bulloch as President of the Executive Council, or Provisional Governor of Georgia, on March 4, 1777. He served only a few months before being defeated for re-election by Governor John A. Treutlen. Politics resulted in a duel in which Gov. Gwinnett was killed by Gen. Lachlan McIntosh on May 16, 1777, and buried in an unknown, unmarked grave. He left so few signatures that one autograph sold for $51,000.

At this writing, the asking price for Gwinnett's autograph has increased from $51,000 to around $200,000, making it one of the most sought-after autographs in the world. According to

Wikipedia, fewer than thirty versions of Gwinnett's original signature are known to exist.

Details of Gwinnett's life are sketchy at best, but some say his unusual first name came from Barbara Button, a cousin who left him a large inheritance. Others say he was named after the fifteenth-century British explorer Sir Thomas Button, who commanded an unsuccessful expedition to find out what happened to explorer Henry Hudson and to navigate the infamous Northwest Passage. The expedition originally consisted of two ships, the *Resolution* and the *Discovery,* but the *Resolution* was lost to sea ice. Button and his party "discovered" and named Mansel Island before returning to England. He is also credited with exploring the west coast of Hudson Bay and naming the area New North Wales and New South Wales.

In his early twenties in England, Button Gwinnett met and married Anne Bourne in 1757. That marriage produced three children: Amelia, Ann, and Elizabeth Ann. About 1762 the family immigrated to the American colonies, first stepping ashore in Charleston, South Carolina, before moving south to Savannah. Apparently he had enough money to purchase St. Catherine's Island, where he became a planter and immersed himself in local politics.

St. Catherine's Island is ten miles long and from one to three miles wide. It consists of more than fourteen thousand acres. Half of the island is dry land, and the other half is covered with ponds and wetlands. Centuries ago it was inhabited by Guale

Indians and was the site of an early Spanish mission. Along with Sapelo and Ossabaw Islands, it eventually passed into the hands of Mary Musgrove and her third husband, the Reverend Thomas Bosomworth. Musgrove, the daughter of an English trader father and a Creek mother, had been the English interpreter for Georgia founder James Oglethorpe. Her first two husbands died. After Mary Musgrove herself died sometime after 1763, her husband sold St. Catherine's to Button Gwinnett in about 1765.

Gwinnett's political life drastically changed in early 1776 when the provincial congress elected him commander of Georgia's Continental battalion. Controversy erupted over this appointment, and Gwinnett stepped down and instead accepted appointment as a Georgia representative to the Second Continental Congress, then meeting in Philadelphia. His successor as Georgia battalion commander was Lachlan McIntosh, a native of Badenoch, Scotland, whose father had moved the family to Georgia in about 1736 with a group of Scottish settlers who founded the town of New Inverness (now known as Darien).

Gwinnett's appointment to the Second Continental Congress assured his place in history after that congress adopted the Declaration of Independence on July 4, 1776. It is a widespread misconception that all the signers of that document affixed their signatures on July 4. In fact, most of the delegates signed the document almost a month later, on August 2.

On July 6, 1775, the Second Provincial Congress of Georgia had accepted the provisions of the Continental Association and had elected five men to represent the state at the Second Continental Congress: John Zubly, John Houstoun, Archibald Bulloch, Noble W. Jones, and Lyman Hall. In February 1776 the list was revised to include Bulloch, Houstoun, Hall, Button Gwinnett, and George Walton. In April the list of representatives was revised again, with Bulloch writing a letter to Hall, Gwinnett, and Walton that gave them great latitude in voting at the Second Continental Congress.

Interestingly, Bulloch fought under the command of Colonel Lachlan McIntosh in the battle of the Rice Boats and the battle of Tybee Island. On June 20, 1776, Bulloch was chosen to become the first president and commander in chief of Georgia under the colony's temporary republican government. His title changed from president to governor of Georgia in 1777.

The Georgia Historical Commission marker at Bulloch's aboveground tomb in Colonial Park Cemetery states:

> Foremost among Georgia's Revolutionary patriots stood Archibald Bulloch whose remains rest in this vault. An early and staunch advocate of American rights, Bulloch was among the patriots who issued the call in 1774 for the first province-wide meeting of the friends of Liberty in Georgia. He served as President of the 1st and the 2nd Provincial Congress & was a delegate in 1775 to the Continental Congress where he won John Adams' praise for his "abilities and fortitude." In April, 1776, Mr. Bulloch became the first President and Commander in Chief of

Georgia, an office he ably filled until his untimely death during the latter part of February, 1777. His loss was a severe blow to the revolutionary cause in Georgia as his was the only leadership which united the Whig factions in the troubled young State. Theodore Roosevelt was the great-great-grandson of the Georgia patriot.

While serving in the Continental Congress, Gwinnett strove to become a brigadier general to lead the First Georgia Regiment. But guess who got the job? None other than his arch-enemy Lachlan McIntosh. Following the war, Gwinnett turned his attention to the creation of Georgia's first state constitution. He wrote the original draft and later became speaker of the Georgia General Assembly.

In February 1777 Archibald Bulloch died unexpectedly (some believe he was poisoned), and the Georgia Council of Safety appointed Gwinnett as Georgia's commander in chief and governor. It would be a short-lived period of service. Gwinnett thought it would be a good idea to fortify and secure Georgia's border with northeastern Florida, which was still controlled by the British. So he directed a military offensive that proved to be disastrous. In the spring of 1777, the General Assembly exonerated Gwinnett of any intentional wrongdoing but still did not reappoint him as commander in chief or governor.

Lachlan McIntosh, who had labeled the ill-fated expedition to Florida as politically motivated, took the opportunity to speak before a session of the new legislature in the spring of 1777 and called Gwinnett "a scoundrel." Those were fighting words to Gwinnett, who demanded that McIntosh restore his honor by accepting the challenge of a duel with pistols.

And so in that meadow on May 16, 1777, McIntosh and Gwinnett faced each other for what would be the very last time. McIntosh's second was Colonel Joseph Habersham. Gwinnett's second was George Wells, a physician.

On April 10, 1914, the *New York Times* reported on a letter being auctioned by the Merwin Company. Written by Wells to Judge John Wereat, it gave Wells's account of the duel:

Late on the evening of Thursday, the 15th [of] May, a written challenge was brought to Genl. McIntosh, signed "Button Gwinnett" wherein the said Mr. Gwinnett charged the General with calling him a scoundrel in Public Convention and desired he would give satisfaction for it a Gentleman before sunrise next morning in Sir James Wright's pasture behind Col Martin's house to which the General humorously sent in answer that the hour was rather earlier than his usual but would assuredly meet him with a pair of Pistols.

Wells then described the "polite salutation" and examination of the pistols that took place that morning. Word of the duel had spread, and a crowd of spectators gathered around, prompting the dueling parties to move farther down a hill. According to Wells, someone suggested that the two should stand back to back. McIntosh replied, "By no means. Let us see what we are about." The account continued:

> Immediately each took his stand and agreed to fire as they could. Both pistols went off nearly at the same time, when Gwinnett fell, being shot about the knee, and said his thigh was broke. The General, who was also shot through the thick of the thigh, stood still in his place, and, noting his antagonist was worse wounded than himself, asked if he had enough or was for another shot, to which all objected. The seconds led the General up to Mr. Gwinnett, and they both shook hands, and, further than this Deponent saith not.

In a later letter from McIntosh to South Carolina Colonel Henry Laurens, McIntosh claimed that Gwinnett's death was in large part due to "the unskillfulness of the doctor," referring to Gwinnett's second, Wells. Apparently Wells also lacked skill as a marksman, because he himself would be shot to death less than three years later in a duel with Major James Jackson in Richmond County, Georgia, near Augusta, in February 1780. It was a tragic ending to a colorful life, since Wells had just become governor of Georgia that same month.

No doubt figuring that it was best to get out of Savannah for a while, McIntosh eventually joined General George Washington at Valley Forge, Pennsylvania, where Washington appointed McIntosh commander of the North Carolina brigade. McIntosh was in Charleston when the British anchored their ships within cannon range and began waiting for the residents to run out of provisions. The British eventually captured the city in May 1780, and McIntosh was taken prisoner. He remained in jail until he was released in a prisoner exchange in February 1782.

Following the war, McIntosh devoted his efforts to building the newly independent Georgia, including helping to organize a treaty with the Indians who occupied the western part of Georgia. He was part of the committee that welcomed George Washington to Savannah in 1791, and McIntosh hosted Washington at his house. McIntosh died on February 20, 1806, and was buried in the Colonial Park Cemetery almost twenty-nine years after his duel with Gwinnett. According to some sources, because of the duel, Gwinnett's wife and daughter, Elizabeth, moved back to Charleston, where they first had arrived in America. His will, dated March 15, 1777, was probated in Chatham County (Savannah) and left his wife and daughter one-half of his "estate in America." The other half he bequeathed to the Reverend Thomas Bosomworth, with whom he had been closely associated.

St. Catherine's Island changed hands several times over the years. One of the owners was automobile executive Howard Coffin, who also owned Sapelo Island. It was Coffin who restored what is believed to have been Gwinnett's house on the north end of St. Catherine's. In 1943 the island passed to New Yorker

Edward John Noble, who cofounded the Life Savers Corporation in 1913 and founded the American Broadcasting Company in 1953 when he purchased the NBC Blue Network. Noble died in December 1958, and ten years later the island was transferred to the Edward J. Noble Foundation, which later conveyed it to the St. Catherine's Island Foundation.

Given today's reverence for the Declaration of Independence, we might think that following the Revolutionary War, monuments would have been erected for all signers of that document. In fact, though, many of them—unlike Thomas Jefferson, John Adams, Ben Franklin, and John Hancock—faded into obscurity. They returned to their lives as farmers, small-town businessmen, and local politicians. And so it was that the exact location of Button Gwinnett's grave simply got lost over the ensuing years.

Stan Denton, senior historian with the Georgia Historical Society in Savannah, observes:

> As to why, it speaks to the fact that until the 1810s and 1820s, folks simply didn't pay much attention to the members of the Revolutionary generation, much like we didn't notice that the World War II vets were important till they all started dying in the 1990s. Then we saw movements for monuments, 50th anniversary celebrations, and movies like *Saving Private Ryan*. Then they became the "Greatest Generation."
>
> The same thing happened to the Founders, at least to all of those not named Washington or Jefferson. It wasn't

till 1818 that the state of Georgia named counties after Gwinnett, Walton, and Hall. The simple fact is, during their own lifetimes, no one thought of them as "founders" or bothered to erect monuments or statues to them.

Denton is convinced that Gwinnett's remains are in Colonial Park Cemetery, even though he doesn't know exactly where:

The location of his grave is one of the great mysteries of American history. My conclusion is based on his death notice in the *Georgia Gazette* newspaper for the day he died, Monday, May 19, 1777. It stated that he had died that morning and would be buried that day in Christ Church cemetery, which is now Colonial Park Cemetery. The exact quote said, "Mr. Gwinnett will be buried before sundown today in Christ Church burial ground." Whether he's actually in the grave that's marked as his in that cemetery is anybody's guess, but if the newspaper is to be believed, he's at least in the cemetery somewhere. The duel took place on Friday when he was shot, and he lingered through the weekend, dying on Monday morning. It's highly likely that he remained in Savannah all through that weekend and was buried in town, as the paper reports. . . . I haven't come across any primary sources written at the time of his death that suggested he was buried anywhere else. Now, that doesn't mean he's not at St. Catherine's, of course, though the contemporary records don't seem to support that.

Denton further observes, to complicate the situation:

Sometime between the time Button Gwinnett died in 1777 and 1848, the marker for BG's grave disappeared, and no one had bothered to put up a new one. And when BG's gravestone disappeared (as have literally hundreds in Colonial Park and indeed in all colonial cemeteries across the country) no one thought it important enough to do anything about it. Now we have no idea exactly where he's buried. That was only discovered—or at any rate brought to the public's attention—when Augusta erected the "Signer's Monument" in 1848, and they wanted to dig up the three signers of the Declaration of Independence from Georgia and bury them there at the monument. They found Walton and Hall but couldn't find BG's grave.

The Signers Monument is now located in the middle of the 600 block of Greene Street. The idea for the monument began when Dr. Louis Alexander Dugas was walking through a field on his Savannah River property near Shell Bluff, about twenty-five miles south of Augusta. He came across an old gravestone that read "Lyman Hall." Dugas's property had been the site of Hall's plantation in his later years. Hall had died in October 1790 at age sixty-six.

Tracking down George Walton's remains was not too much trouble. Walton had died in 1804 at age sixty-four at his Meadow Garden home near 13th Street and Walton Way (named after the signer) in Augusta. He was buried in Rosney Cemetery. The coffin of what was believed to be George Walton was unearthed, and inside was the skeleton of a man of the right size and approximate age with the remains of a musket ball lodged in a thigh bone.

When the cornerstone was laid on the Fourth of July of 1848, the monument wasn't yet called the Signers Monument, and Button Gwinnett was not even mentioned by name in local newspaper articles about the obelisk.

In 1956 Gwinnett's name was finally included as part of the monument by the placement of a Georgia Historical Commission marker. It reads:

> Dedicated July 4, 1848, in honor of the signers of the Declaration of Independence for Georgia: George Walton, Lyman Hall and Button Gwinnett. The first two lie buried in crypts beneath this shaft. The burial place of Gwinnett, whose body was to have been re-interred here, has never been found.
>
> George Walton, born in Virginia, settled in Georgia, and was a colonel in the Revolutionary Army, twice governor of Georgia, judge of Superior Court and chief justice of Georgia, six times elected to Congress and served one term as United States Senator; wounded and captured by British at Savannah.

Dr. Lyman Hall, born in Connecticut, was one of the group of ardent revolutionaries from Midway, Georgia, who helped lead Georgia into open rebellion in 1776. He represented Georgia in the Continental Congress.

Button Gwinnett, born in England, settled in Savannah shortly before the Revolution and was a magnetic and fiery figure in the early days of the war. He was president of Georgia in March 1777. A quarrel with General Lachlan McIntosh, arising out of the ill-fated expedition to Florida, resulted in a duel in May 1777, on the outskirts of Savannah in which Gwinnett was mortally wounded.

The mystery continues as to the actual whereabouts of the remains of this Declaration of Independence signer. May you rest in peace, Button Gwinnett, wherever you may be.

CHAPTER 12

THE GOLD AND SILVER OF THE CONFEDERACY

Most Americans know that the Civil War officially ended with the surrender of Confederate General Robert E. Lee to Union General Ulysses S. Grant in the two-story home of Wilmer McLean at Appomattox Court House, Virginia, on April 9, 1865. By that time, the Confederate government was in shambles, and its leaders were trying to save themselves. Jefferson Davis, president of the Confederacy, fled the Confederate capital of Richmond, Virginia, and headed into the Deep South in an ultimately futile escape attempt. His flight also put in motion a mystery that endures to this day: What happened to the gold and silver bars in the Confederate treasury that today would be worth millions of dollars?

Many believe that the gold and silver ingots are buried somewhere around Washington, Georgia, where Davis presided over the last meeting of the Confederate cabinet. Others believe they are buried in the Savannah River. Still others believe that they were stolen by unknown raiders who deposited them in foreign banks.

The missing bullion dates back to a meeting between Confederate Vice President Alexander H. Stephens of Crawfordville, Virginia, and his old friend, President Abraham Lincoln. As the southern states were overrun by Yankee troops, Stephens made a last attempt to work out a solution by which the South could remain an independent, separate nation. He arranged to meet with Lincoln on board Lincoln's steamer boat off Hampton Roads, Virginia, on February 3, 1865. The two had been friends since Lincoln's freshman term in Congress in 1848.

In his book *Alexander H. Stephens of Georgia: A Biography*, Thomas E. Schott writes: "Once the meeting settled down to business, it became apparent that Lincoln would not be budged. Restoration of the Union and an end to the rebellion was the only basis on which he would entertain discussion. Stephens tried several times to explore the question of an armistice to allow a cooling off period and possible joint effort against the French in Mexico."

The four-hour-long meeting, known as the Hampton Roads Conference, had no significant results, except that Lincoln did agree to consider Stephens's request to free the vice president's nephew, Confederate Lieutenant John A. Stephens, who had been captured at the fall of Port Hudson.

According to Schott, Lincoln later freed the young officer and sent him home with a note to his uncle asking that the nephew be exchanged for a Union prisoner of equal rank whose physical condition required an immediate release. Lincoln, in an extremely

This cylindrical painting of one of the final Civil War battles in Atlanta can be found at Grant Park in Atlanta.

COURTESY OF GEORGIA DEPARTMENT OF ECONOMIC DEVELOPMENT

unusual gesture, also gave the young officer a photo of himself and autographed it: "Don't have these where you're from."

Three months after his meeting with Lincoln, Stephens, realizing that all was lost, went to his Liberty Hall plantation outside Crawfordville to wait for the Union soldiers to come and arrest him.

President Davis, however, was not going to let the end come that easily. The news of Lee's surrender on April 9 was slow in coming to the South, whose communications lines had been severely damaged. *The Daily Chronicle & Sentinel* in Augusta, Georgia, told its readers on April 18:

Our city was filled with rumors yesterday. One to the effect that Gen. Lee and his whole army had been captured. Another was that Gen. Lee had made peace. We do not believe either rumor. We think they were started by speculators to affect prices. Our people should be slow to believe all they hear on the streets. The facts are bad enough without their being exaggerated.

It wasn't until April 23 that the *Chronicle* finally published Lee's "General Order No. 9." Lee wrote:

After four years of arduous service, marked by unsurpassed courage and fortitude, the Army of Northern Virginia has been compelled to yield to overwhelming numbers and resources.

I need not tell the brave survivors of so many hard fought battles; who have remained steadfast to the last, that I have consented to this result from no distrust of them. But feeling that valor and devotion could accomplish nothing that could compensate for the loss that would have attended the continuance of the contest, I determine to avoid the useless sacrifice of those whose past services have endeared them to the countrymen.

By the terms of the agreement, officers and men can return to their homes and remain until exchanged. You will take with you the satisfaction that proceeds from the consciousness of duty, faithfully performed, and I earnestly pray that a merciful God will extend to you his blessing and protection.

With an unceasing admiration of your constancy and devotion to your country, and a grateful remembrance of your kind and generous consideration for myself, I bid you an affectionate farewell.

R. E. Lee, General

At war's end, thousands of impoverished and hungry Confederate soldiers in tattered uniforms began heading home, where they faced a bleak future. Apparently, this mass migration resulted in the decision to turn over the Confederate gold to Union army officials, to be used to help out returning Confederate soldiers. That responsibility fell to Confederate Major Rafael Jacob Moses, a lawyer and fifth-generation South Carolinian. Before the war Moses had moved to Columbus, Georgia, and pioneered the commercial growing of plums and peaches in what would become known as the "Peach State."

In a speech to the Civil War Roundtable in Washington, Georgia, in 2007, Lewis Regenstein detailed Moses's important role in the transportation of the Confederate bullion, whose worth he estimated at $750,000 in today's dollars. He noted that Moses was the commissary officer under the command of Confederate General James Longstreet and was responsible "for supplying and feeding up to 54,000 troops, porters and other non-combatants."

Moses was ordered to head for Washington, where Varina Davis was awaiting her husband along with "a train containing gold and silver bullion." General Joseph E. Johnston ordered Moses to provide 250,000 rations at Augusta for the returning soldiers and to meet with Union Major General Edward L. Molineux, occupying commander of Augusta, to arrange for federal troops to protect Moses in his mission. Moses was also ordered to do what he could for Confederate sick and wounded in hospitals.

Accounts differ, but it seems that, out of the Confederate treasury's last $40,000 in bullion, Moses paid $10,000 to the quartermaster-general in Washington, Georgia, and transported the remaining $30,000 to Augusta.

Several years after the war, Captain M. H. Clark of Clarksville, Tennessee, who had been the acting secretary of the Confederate treasury, wrote to Jefferson Davis. Clark said that he had been directed to turn the silver bullion over to Major Moses. As Clark also stated, he personally saw Moses put the bullion into a warehouse in Washington and directed Moses to burn the Confederate notes in the presence of himself and the Confederacy's secretary of war, General John C. Breckinridge.

In 1882 Clark told the *Louisville Courier-Journal*:

Before reaching town [Washington, Georgia], I was halted by Major R. J. Moses, to turn over to him the specie [treasury money] which president Davis, before he left, ordered to be placed at the disposal of the Commissary Department, to feed the paroled soldiers and stragglers passing through, to prevent their burdening a section already stripped of supplies. I turned over to Major Moses the wagons and silver bullion and all of the escort except [for] about ten men.

Moses knew that word was spreading quickly about the gold and silver bullion left in his charge, and he knew there were many desperate people in the South, including soldiers, who wanted those riches for themselves. Because of his concern about the security of the bullion, General Robert Toombs gave Moses the names of ten members of the Washington Artillery who could be trusted to help safeguard the shipment.

Moses later wrote in his unpublished memoirs:

I agreed to pay them $10.00 each in gold to guard it that night and go with me to Augusta. I then took a squad of them and destroyed all the liquor I could find in the shops. I then got part of a keg of powder and put it in a wooden building that was unoccupied and put the boxes of bullion in the same room, placed my guard outside and around the building, and gave out that I had laid a train of powder to the outside, and if the guard was forced, the train would be fired.

Not long after the treasury train was under way to Augusta with some two hundred soldiers and twenty-nine cavalrymen, the conductor approached Moses and said there was a rumor that the train might be attacked at Barnett, Georgia. As it turned out, the conductor was correct, and Moses and his security detail were faced by a mob determined to get their hands on the gold and silver bars.

In his book *The History of the State of Georgia from 1850–1881*, I. W. Avery recounts that Moses went out among the mob, "who were as thick as blackbirds," and told them that every dollar of the bullion would be devoted to feeding their fellow soldiers and caring for the wounded in Augusta's hospitals.

Moses said that if the mob killed him and his guard, they would be killing "men in the discharge of a duty in behalf of their comrades—that if they killed us, it would be murder while, if we killed any of them in defending the bullion which we certainly should endeavor to do, we would be justified, because the killing would be in self defense and in a discharge of a sacred duty." Two soldiers in the crowd apparently spoke up and vouched for Moses, causing the crowd to disperse for a while. Moses was warned that some men were about to charge the boxcar. This time a young man from Tennessee with a wound on his cheek showed "remarkable courage" in averting the charge.

According to Lewis Regenstein, Moses and his men were finally able to deliver their precious cargo to Augusta, where he obtained a receipt of delivery from Quartermaster/Major R. R. Wood dated May 5, 1865.

In 1927 *The Atlanta Journal* published an article telling of Moses's action. The article, titled "Last Official Writing of the Southern Confederacy," reproduced the receipt, calling it "the last official writing ever issued by the Confederate administration." In his unpublished memoirs, Moses gives this account:

> When we reached Augusta the banks were afraid to take charge of the bullion. I applied unsuccessfully to Metcalf's bank. I then went to General Mollyneux [sic], to explain to him my mission, got a guard from him and had the bullion carried to the Commissary's office in Augusta.
>
> The next day, I met the Tennessean [from the train] & told him I was glad he was in Augusta, as it would enable me to show him that I had no interest in the specie except for the benefit of the soldiers as required in my orders. He went with me to Governor [Alfred] Cummings, formerly Gov of Utah. We met General Mollyneux at his office. He agreed to receive the silver and gold, ration the troops as they passed through, appropriate $2,000 to the hospitals, and at his request I wrote the correspondence on both sides.
>
> He signed one in duplicate and I the other, and he faithfully fulfilled his contract. I never knew whether the U.S. Government got the bullion or not [that] I delivered to a Mass. Provost Marshall by Mollyneux's order. I tried afterwards to trace it into the Treasury and left all the papers with Jerry Black of Penn. He was, I think, Johnson's attorney general. James Waddell was with me when I delivered the papers but I have never heard anything about the bullion.

Backing up Moses's account is the firsthand testimony of the Reverend R. H. Fleming, pastor of Westminster Presbyterian Church in Richmond, Virginia, which was published in *The Augusta Chronicle* on June 8, 1904. Fleming was one of the Confederate naval cadets from the training ship *Patrick Henry* who guarded the Confederate archives and treasury on their trip from Richmond to Augusta after Richmond was evacuated.

This is Fleming's account, as originally published in the *Richmond Times-Dispatch* newspaper:

We left our quarters at the tobacco factory at 4 p.m. on Sunday and proceeded rapidly to the Danville [Virginia] depot. On reaching it, we were formed in line and were addressed by Captain Lowell, the commandant of midshipmen, who told us that we had been selected by the secretary because he believed us to be brave, honest and discreet young officers and gentlemen, for a service of particular danger and delicacy; that to our guardianship was to be committed a valuable train containing the archives of the government with its money. We were then marched into the depot where our train in company with others was receiving freight. Guards were placed at all entrances and the squad with fixed bayonets cleared the building of loafers and citizens.

This train left the depot at midnight and two midshipmen, with loaded revolvers, were placed in each car containing the government boxes; one to sleep while

140

the other watched. In those cars also were government clerks with several ladies, their wives and their personal baggage. The next day we reached Danville and on the 5th of April Admiral [Raphael] Semmes with the men of the James River Squadron (the ironclad had been blown up on the night of the 20th) reached the point and were assigned to its defense. Midshipman Semmes was here detailed to his father's staff, and Midshipman Breckinridge accompanied his father (secretary of war) as his personal aid [sic]. Our train stood on the track not far from the depot and our encampment was in a grove not far from the train.

On the 9th of April, we left Danville and reached Greensboro, N.C., about 4 p.m. the 10th; then on to Charlotte. While there the money was placed in the mint and the midshipmen feasted at the leading hotels. On the 13th, we were off for Chester, S.C. Here the government's specie, papers, treasury clerks and their wives, etc., were placed in wagons for a march across country to the railroad at Newberry [South Carolina]. I saw the cargo transferred to the wagons and there were small, square boxes which we supposed contained gold or bullion and kegs resembling beer kegs which we inferred contained silver.

The train was not a long one. Mrs. [Jefferson] Davis and child and nurse occupied a large ambulance. I do not know whether she joined us at Greensboro or Charlotte. We marched to Newberry reaching there on the 15th of April and the same day took care for Abbeville [South Carolina]. Left Abbeville with wagon train on the 17th and reached Washington, Ga., on the 19th. We went to Augusta, Ga., on the 20th and here the money was placed in the vaults of a bank. Some of it. I know not how much was sold to citizens; at least men crowded around with Confederate currency to get gold. On the 24th we were ordered back to Washington, Ga. "the things" going with us. [It seems the "middies" had playfully dubbed the specie boxes "the things."]

On the 27th the midshipmen who desired them were offered furloughs which were accepted by all but five Virginians—Quarles, Hudson, Slaughter, Carter and Fleming. "The things" were again put in wagons and across the country we marched on the 29th of April to Abbeville, S.C., where "the things" were put on board some cars that stood at the depot. We had no guard duty to do after leaving Washington, Ga.

On May 2, President Davis and staff and cabinet reached Abbeville, coming I imagined from Charlotte on horseback. On that day we five Virginians were discharged, as per the following order, probably the last official act of the navy of the Confederate states: "Abbeville, S.C., May 2, 1865. Sir: You are hereby detached from the

Naval School and leave is granted you to visit your home. You will report by letter to the honorable secretary of the navy as soon as practicable. Paymaster Wheless will issue you ten days' rations and quartermasters are requested to furnish you transportation. Respectfully, your obedient servant. WILLIAM H. PARKER, Commanding."

So what really happened to the treasure? Who will ever know for sure?

We do know that on May 21, 1865, Confederacy President Jefferson Davis and Confederacy Vice President Alexander H. Stephens were brought as prisoners to Augusta. Accompanying them were Davis's wife, their two children, and Mrs. Davis's sister; prisoner Clement C. Clay, a Confederate States senator from Alabama, and his wife; and prisoners General John H. Reagan (the Confederacy's postmaster), former Texas governor Frank R. Lubbock, and Confederate General Joseph Wheeler and his staff.

Davis and his guard, Colonel Benjamin Pritchard, had a "comfortable" dinner with General Molineaux, the military commander of Augusta. Then Molineaux sent the entire group of distinguished prisoners on a boat down the Savannah River to the port of Savannah, where the men were transferred to a larger ship taking them to northern prisons.

We also know that just days before the distinguished Confederate prisoners arrived in Augusta, something else quite valuable arrived in the city.

The May 17, 1865, edition of the *Chronicle & Sentinel* reported that Brigadier General Cuvier Grover, commandant of the District of Savannah, and his staff had arrived in Augusta the day before by steamer boat from Savannah. Among the members of his staff was Provost Marshal Lieutenant Colonel Robert P. York.

"Gen. Grover is the guest of Gen. Molineaux," the newspaper article reported. "We learn that he will be in the city several days. We trust his visit will be a pleasant one and that our citizens will show him the attention he deserves."

On May 25, 1865, the *New York Times* told the real reason that General Grover and his staff had traveled to Augusta:

AUGUSTA, Wednesday, May 17, 3:30 P.M. Lieut. Col. [Robert P.] York, Provost Marshal on Gen. Grover's staff, has had turned over to him, and will take to Savannah today, $243,000 of gold and silver, seized as property of the Confederate government. $488,000 was taken from a Confederate baggage wagon found in a by-road, and the balance was taken from various parties who had it in trust but acknowledged that it belonged to the Confederate government. Col. York will also take some millions of dollars in Confederate bonds and currency, enough to start a small paper-mill.

This account is further supported by another article in the *New York Times* on June 17, 1883. According to the article,

Robert York, who was then living in De Ruyter, New York, had in his possession a vast amount of Confederate correspondence and other written materials. York, who had been a lieutenant colonel of the Seventy-fifth New York Volunteers, had accompanied the Second Division of the Nineteenth Army Corps from the Shenandoah Valley to Savannah in December 1864.

The *Times* article reports:

> A few days after the arrival of Gen. Grover's (Second) division of the Nineteenth Corps at Savannah, Col. York was appointed Provost Marshal of the district and acted in that capacity until his muster-out [of the army] . . .
>
> . . . The most interesting and important documents preserved by Col. York are the receipts given him by various authorities for immense amounts of gold and silver coin bullion received by him from the Provost Marshal at Augusta.
>
> The receipt of John W. Pollock, First Lieutenant and Assistant Provost Marshal-General, Department of the South, dated June 12, 1865, is Col. York's voucher for the transfer to that officer, besides the official records of Gen. [G. T.] Beauregard of Confederate notes and bonds to the amount of $8,980,241.
>
> The receipt of Albert A. G. Brown, Special Agent of the Treasury Department, dated June 10, 1865, is Col. York's voucher for the transfer to him of 16 kegs and two boxes containing gold and silver coin to the amount

(by actual count) of $61,440.30, and also five boxes containing gold and silver bullion to the quantity (actual weight) of 11,089 penny-weights of gold and 144,400 penny-weights of silver.

The receipt of W. B. Johnston and several others, officers of the Georgia Bank and Railroad Company, shows the transfer by them to Col. York of four kegs said to contain $121,295.65, besides one trunk and 30 boxes, the property of various corporations and persons of Savannah, which had been deposited in the vaults of the Georgia Bank for safe keeping.

In regard to all these receipts in Colonel York's possession, the *New York Times* article concluded:

The amount of cash and bullion actually counted and weighed and turned over to the United States Treasury Agent, with the enormous figure of Confederate notes and bonds also turned over, is prima facie evidence that this was the remnant of the Confederate Treasury at Richmond, which took its flight southward with the Jeff Davis party when Grant overran the defenses of Petersburg in the first week of April 1865. As the *New York Times* reported in its articles about Colonel York and Major Moses, that lost gold and silver wasn't really lost after all.

CHAPTER 13

PASAQUAN AND OTHER UNUSUAL PLACES

Many mysterious houses and other places can be found throughout Georgia. Some are mysterious because of supernatural occurrences, such as objects moving for unexplained reasons or ghostly apparitions of former residents who met violent deaths. Other houses are mysterious because they are so unusually built and designed that they raise questions as to how they came into being. Most communities also have their own unique characters, and Eddie Owens Martin, who lived in an unusual home outside the small town of Buena Vista in southwest Georgia, certainly was a unique character.

Martin lived in an 1880s farmhouse on four acres of sandy land that he had inherited from his mother. When he drove his bright-red Ford station wagon into town, he would be wearing a turban, sometimes a cape, brightly colored robes, black pants with bells on the side, and beads in his beard. Even in mid-1980s Georgia, that attire attracted the attention of local residents and visitors, most of whom just accepted Martin as the local eccentric.

Martin, one of five children, was born on July 4, 1908. His parents were farmers in Marion County. He left home in his teens, partly because of his father's cruelty but mostly because he just wanted to see what else was out there in the world.

Eventually he made his way to New York City, where he survived by becoming a male prostitute, a drag queen, a waiter, and a fortune-teller, and by selling home-cooked soul food to southerners in the Big Apple. He immersed himself in the free art galleries and museums and explored his creative nature. He came to believe that man had strayed from his natural path and needed the wisdom of ancient civilizations to survive. That belief was supported by visions Martin saw of tall creatures with large hair who guided his spiritual journey.

Upon the death of his mother, Martin inherited the family's farmhouse and in 1957 moved back permanently to Buena Vista. He combed his long hair into an upswept look that he depicted in his many paintings. Martin believed that his hair, which he never cut, was an antenna to his spiritual world. He then began using his visions and artistic talents to reinvent himself as St. EOM (Eddie Owens Martin), the high priest presiding over his small domain that he called Pasaquan. The name Pasaquan apparently came from the Spanish word *pasa* (meaning "to pass") and the Asian word *quoyan,* used to describe bringing the past and future together.

The house and property—with its brightly painted concrete, carved wood, and hammered aluminum creations—is a

Visitors from afar are amazed while touring St. EOM's unusual house, decorated throughout with brightly painted concrete, wood carvings, and hammered aluminum.

Technicolor marvel that Walt Disney might have been proud to own, if it weren't for the huge St. EOM–created male and female figures with their overly endowed private parts.

On April 16, 1986, less than four months before what would have been his seventy-eighth birthday, Martin put a .38-caliber pistol to his right temple and pulled the trigger. He was tired of his increasing medical ailments and apparently of this world of human souls. His suicide note read: "No one is to blame but me and my past."

And yet in death, Martin's legend and fame keep growing thanks to the farmhouse and its improvements, which he bequeathed to the Marion County Historical Society. Around 1992 the organization created the Pasaquan Preservation Society and turned the house into a historic site open for public tours most months of the year.

In 2008 Pasaquan was placed on the National Register of Historic Places. Every Fourth of July, which is also Martin's birthday, Pasaquan hosts the St. EOM Birthday and Independence Celebration.

Besides the eye-catching house of Eddie Owens Martin, Georgia is home to several other extremely unusual places.

Tommy Scott's Asian-Inspired Home

Just south of Toccoa in northeastern Georgia—not far from where James Brown began his musical career and baseball legend Ty Cobb was born and reared—is an extremely unusual Asian-inspired house that has been the focus of national and international attention. It has been featured twice on the HGTV cable network's popular *Extreme Homes* program and its *Offbeat America* series, and once in an episode of Charles Kuralt's *On the Road* series on the CBS network.

"I thought it was interesting why an older man in the United States would want an Asian-themed home," the program's researcher and caster Rezal Turner told *Toccoa Record* reporter Christine Brubaker. "When a home is so interesting and unique, it must reflect on the owner." The HGTV network sent film crews from Nashville and Colorado to Toccoa for the filming.

What makes the home so interesting and unique is that its creators, country music entertainers Frankie and Tommy Scott, have never been to Asia. So the mystery is: Why did they go to such elaborate lengths to build this Asian-style home in rural Georgia and decorate it with Asian furnishings if they had never been to the Far East?

First you have to know what a zest for life this couple had in the more than sixty years of marriage they shared before Frankie's death at age eighty-four in 2004. For decades the twosome criss-crossed America and Canada as the owners and stars of what they called "the last real medicine show," which combined old-style country music with vaudeville-style entertainment. Guest stars who traveled with the show and its more than one hundred employees, who traveled in a caravan of seven vehicles, included such western movie legends as Tim McCoy, Al "Fuzzy" St. John, Lash LaRue, Johnny Mack Brown, and Sunset "Kit" Carson.

"We did performances almost seven days a week for sixty-five years," the semiretired Tommy said. "I figure we did about 29,000 engagements." He was inducted into the Country Music Hall of Fame's Walkway of Stars section and has been interviewed by David Letterman, Johnny Carson, Ralph Emery, Oprah Winfrey, and Charles Kuralt.

Although such trips were rare, the Scotts returned each year to their large, Asian-themed house in Toccoa to recharge their batteries and take a break from the show-business world. As of this writing, Tommy, now in his nineties, still lives there.

The one-story house resembles a Chinese pagoda, and every room has a Chinese theme. Most of the features were designed by Tommy himself. Sandra Whitworth, the Scotts' daughter, said the idea for the house began forming when the Scotts were living in California in the late 1940s and early 1950s, when Sandra was little.

"We spent a lot of time around Los Angeles," Whitworth recalled. "Mother would buy a few Oriental pieces here and there to do an Oriental bedroom and living room when there was a place where she could put them. Mother had an eye for good things. She was a model when she and daddy got married, and she worked as a model for Rich's department store in Atlanta modeling clothes to show women lunching in the tea room on the glass bridge."

Whitworth said the unusual house began as a double-wide trailer out in the country. Then the large Old West room was added in the 1950s to house the Scotts' growing collection of show-business memorabilia from their connections to western movies, circuses, and country music shows. Today the room is covered from ceiling to floor with photos, newspaper clippings, and memorabilia from Tommy's many years in music, movies, and stage shows. He starred in a full-length western movie titled *Trail of the Hawk* and was also featured in a number of musical movie shorts.

"The flower room with the small bridge and waterfall [was] added about 1963 or 1964," Whitworth said. "My daddy painted the mural in that room. He had painted fireplace screens when he was a teenager in high school and sold them around the area. That's how he got his spending money. And when he graduated from high school, he wanted to go to an art school in Atlanta. But his father told him that he didn't know how his son could make a living at painting or picking a guitar and those were the only two things my daddy really knew how to do."

Every two or three years, the Scotts built another major addition to the house that carried out the Asian theme. And every Christmas, they decorated their home with thousands of lights.

"They'd turn them on two weeks before Christmas," Whitfield said. "That's how a lot of the local people saw the place for the first time. They'd hear about the many lights and go see them, and there would be this Oriental house out in the middle of nowhere."

So, given the Scotts' love of the Far East, why didn't they ever take a vacation or working trip there?

"Part of that is a fear of flying," Whitworth said, "and it's an awfully long trip to Asia and back on a boat."

For most of his show-business career, Tommy Scott portrayed the role of an old medicine show salesman and sold bottles of herbal cures. He often noted that herbal medicine began with the Chinese, and he felt that his house should reflect that Asian culture. The old medicine show wagon that he used as a prop has been on display in the Georgia Music Hall of Fame in Macon since that building opened in 1996.

Some people who make it to ninety have trouble just breathing, but Scott at ninety was promoting his seven-hundred-page autobiography, called *Snake Oil, Super Stars, and Me* (co-authored by Randall Franks and Shirley Noe Swiesz), and making plans for his one hundredth birthday.

"Most people guess that I'm about seventy-two or in my late seventies," Scott said a couple of years ago when he turned ninety. "I just think young, and I don't eat half as much as most people. I am six feet and weigh 145 pounds. I went for a checkup a couple of weeks ago, and my doctor said, 'I can't find one thing wrong with you. Just keep on doing what you've been doing.'

"I told my doctor that I know that I'm going to get to be one hundred, and he said, 'If you do, there is going to be a big fight that day.' I said, 'What do you mean?' and he said, 'It will be a big fight between you and Jesus arguing if you're going to be around another ten years.'"

Lapham-Patterson House in Thomasville

In Thomasville, Georgia, stands a six-thousand-square-foot house with nineteen rooms, forty-five doors, and fifty-three windows.

Twenty-five of the doors open to the outside, giving each room an exit. Each of the windows opens from both the bottom up and the top down. All the rooms, except for the servants' work area, open to either a porch or a balcony. In this Queen Anne–style Victorian-era home, none of the rooms are alike, and none are square or rectangular. The residence was the first private home in Thomasville to have closets, more than one bathroom, hot and cold running water, and a self-contained gas lighting system.

So, what is the history behind this unusual house, which was constructed in 1885?

As a teenager, Charles Willard Lapham survived the Great Chicago Fire of 1871 but suffered damage to his lungs. As an adult he prospered in the shoe business in Chicago while continuing to search for a place that would improve his health. That search led to Thomasville, where he built a two-story "winter cottage" at 626 North Dawson St. Just over a year after the house was built, the March 25, 1887, edition of *The Augusta Chronicle,* in an article profiling Thomasville, took note of Lapham's house.

"Mr. C. W. Lapham of Chicago is the possessor of a home on Dawson Street which for architectural beauty and design is not surpassed by any private residence in the state," the article noted. "The house is surrounded by beautiful water oaks, and the fountains, which are scattered here and there over the lawn, give a freshness to the scene."

Lapham owned the house for about ten years. In early 1894 James Larmon, owner of the Cincinnati Barbed Wire Fence Company, purchased it. Unfortunately, Larmon suffered heart problems and died in December 1904. In 1905 the house was purchased by James G. Patterson Jr., a turpentine business owner from North Carolina who had moved his business and family to south Georgia. The house stayed in the Patterson family until the city of Thomasville acquired it in 1970. In 1974 it was opened as a public museum. The house is listed on the National Register of Historic Places.

Paradise Gardens in Summerville

One man's junk is another man's treasure. Nowhere is that saying truer than at the World's Folk Art Chapel (in Paradise Gardens in Summerville, Georgia, two blocks off GA 27 North), which is constructed of cast-off and recycled materials. In fact, all of the artistic creations in a maze of structures and sculptures were made from bottles, glass, mirrors, cement, bathtubs, toilets, rusted bicycle frames, cast-off cheap jewelry, and just about anything else once regarded as useless.

But these creations of folk artist and preacher Howard Finster have attracted visitors worldwide as well as the attention of the Library of Congress, the Smithsonian Institution, *The Wall Street Journal,* and other upper-crust organizations. Johnny Carson interviewed Finster on the *Tonight Show with Johnny Carson,* a late-night TV program. Coca-Cola commissioned Finster to paint an eight-foot Olympic Coke bottle to represent the U.S. art exhibit for the 1996 Summer Olympics in Atlanta. The rock group R.E.M. worked with him to design the cover of their second album, *Reckoning,* and filmed the video for their song "Radio Free Europe" in Paradise Gardens Park and Museum. The country music group Blackhawk likewise filmed the video for their song "That's Just About Right" at Paradise Gardens.

Like Eddie Owens Martin, Howard Finster had visions that told him, at age fifty-nine, that painting would be his vehicle for spreading his spiritual messages to the world.

"Visual art is a great thing," Finster was quoted as saying. "It draws the attention of people. That's what people's work does. It preaches for them after they're gone."

The story goes that in 1976 Finster was rubbing paint on a bicycle with his fingers when he saw a face on one of his fingers and heard a voice telling him to do sacred art. Finster protested that he was not a professional painter, only to have the voice ask simply, "How do you know?"

By the time Finster died on October 23, 2001, at age eighty-four, he had completed more than forty-six thousand pieces of original art. He died one day short of the sixty-sixth anniversary of his marriage to his wife, Pauline. They had five children.

CHAPTER 14

CIRCUS IN THE CEMETERY

Circuses can be full of mysteries: The clowns hide their true identities behind lots of garish makeup, and the performers who have run away to join the circus are often hiding past lives.

Visitors to cemeteries in Moultrie and Columbus, Georgia, will find two interesting mysteries relating to the circus: unusual circus-inspired gravestones. Visitors might be left wondering: Why are those gravestones there, and what are the stories behind them?

At Pleasant Grove Primitive Baptist Church in Moultrie on GA 37 leading to Adel, visitors encounter a life-size baby elephant of white stone with its trunk held high. But who placed it there, and why is it in this church cemetery?

The elephant actually marks two graves: that of circus owner William F. Duggan, who was born on January 18, 1899, and died on December 22, 1950; and that of his father, George Duggan, who was born on November 1, 1856, and died on October 4, 1902.

I located Stancel "Stan" May, nephew of William Duggan, in Jonesboro, Georgia. His mother, Beauford, was Duggan's sister. May confirmed that at an early age his uncle ran away and joined the Sparks Circus, originally working with elephants. About 1934 Duggan created the Duggan Bros. circus, even though no brother of his was involved. According to May, the circus was on the road for only about one year. Then, for most of the 1930s and 1940s, Duggan turned his business attention to jukeboxes and slot machines in Florida.

In the late 1940s Duggan and his son, William F. Duggan Jr., and his nephew May took their Pan American Worldwide Animal Exhibit on the road for a number of years. They were in the process of developing this show into the three-ring Hagen-Wallace Circus when Duggan died of a heart attack in Deland, Florida. His son did take the Hagen-Wallace show on the road for several years before opening an amusement park at Fort Walton Beach, Florida.

One of the animals that Duggan Bros. owner William F. Duggan had acquired in 1949 was a baby elephant that he named Nancy, after his son's daughter. After Duggan's death his son decided to honor his father with the sculpture of Nancy. The granite statue was carved by the Tate Marble Company in north Georgia.

The sculpture is 5 feet 6 inches tall, 7 feet 2 inches long, and 2 feet 4 inches thick. It rests on a pink Etowah marble base that is 8 feet long, 7 feet wide, and 6 inches thick.

An unusual gravestone memorial in the shape of a circus tent
commemorates circus workers who lost their lives in a head-on train
accident near Columbus, Georgia.

The elephant in the Moultrie church cemetery is not the
only circus-themed gravestone to arouse visitors' curiosity. So does
a mysterious monument in Riverdale Cemetery in Columbus. The
large monument resembles a small circus tent, with a peaked top
and ruffles on the edges. The inscription on the side reads:

Erected By The

Con T Kennedy Shows

In Memory Of Their Comrades

Who Lost Their Lives

In A Railroad Wreck Near Columbus, Ga.

Nov. 22, 1915

So, what happened to this train? Why did those circus people lose their lives?

The tragedy, which killed at least six people and sent more than forty to area hospitals, took place on a Monday afternoon as the Con T. Kennedy Carnival Company train was six and a half miles east of Columbus and had almost reached its destination of Phenix City, Alabama, just across the state line.

Jan Page, who features the wreck on her Web site (www .angelfire.com/weird2/georgia/page4.html), writes: "Judging from what I have read, the accident occurred near the Bull Creek bridge. I think I have found this bridge. It can be seen from what is now Macon Road. It is near where the crime lab and driver's license office is. It appears to be ornate and mostly white. It is a pretty, old looking structure."

The Kennedy carnival just had finished a successful engagement at the Georgia Harvest Festival in Atlanta. The formal inquest proved that the accident was the fault of conductor J. W. Reichert and engineer J. L. Fickling, who were operating a Central of Georgia Railroad passenger train. They had disobeyed instructions to wait at the Muscogee Junction siding until the carnival train, which was heading in the opposite direction, had passed.

When they hit head-on, both trains were going about thirty miles per hour. The engines of both trains were demolished but did not leave the tracks. According to the *Columbus Ledger* newspaper, two carloads of animals managed to stay intact.

"Down the tracks, where the long string of carnival cars were standing unhurt, were cars of wild animals, and the roars of the lions, panthers and bears brought a shudder to the throngs gathered, causing the thought of what would happen if they had been allowed to escape," the newspaper observed.

The twelve Pullman cars at the rear of the train, which carried the top carnival employees, received little damage. The front cars on both trains sustained the most damage. All of the six known dead were on the carnival train.

A front-page article published the next day said:

Fred S. Kempf and his wife were burned to death while show people looked helplessly on. Their 4-year-old child [Hazel] was saved through the heroism of her mother alone. Flames were licking at one of the palatial automobile trucks of the Kempfs, which was on a flat car and in which the Kempfs were imprisoned. Mrs. Kempf, seeing that there was no chance to escape, hurled her child through a window, clear of the train. Then the mother fell back and was burned alive a minute later.

The child was badly bruised, but Columbus people who picked up the little girl and rushed her to a hospital say that the little girl will live.

Also among the dead were a Kennedy showman known only as "Whitey" and carnival workers George Johnson of San Francisco and Milton Andrews of Lexington, Kentucky. They were buried in Riverdale Cemetery. The bodies of Mr. and Mrs. Kempf were sent to their hometown of Capac, Michigan, near Grand Rapids.

Carnival owner Con T. Kennedy said the actual number of dead probably would never be known since many of the hired laborers were not listed on his books and their bodies might have been destroyed in the burning cars.

On Thanksgiving Day of 1915, the women of Columbus served Thanksgiving dinner to the carnival's employees. Then, after borrowing equipment from different carnival companies that had closed for the season, the Con T. Kennedy Carnival Company opened its engagement in Phenix City. As the saying goes, the show must go on.

BIBLIOGRAPHY

Elberton's Stonehenge and Dutchy

Bradford, Bill. "Old Statue Gets a Lift from Grave." *The Augusta Chronicle,* April 25, 1982.

Miles, Jim. *Weird Georgia: Close Encounters, Strange Creatures, and Unexplained Phenomena.* Nashville, TN: Cumberland House Publishing, 2000.

Schemmel, William. *Georgia Curiosities: Quirky Characters, Roadside Oddities, and Other Offbeat Stuff.* Guilford, CT: Globe Pequot Press, 2003.

United Press International. "Mysterious Stonehenge Erected in Elberton." *The Augusta Chronicle,* March 24, 1980.

The Real "Eve" and Her Three Faces

Gibson, Iris. "Eve Puts Faces, Lives behind Her." *The Augusta Chronicle,* July 29, 1981.

Harrison, Tom. "Eve Reflects on Past." *The Augusta Chronicle,* January 14, 1975.

Owens, Gene. "Aikenite's Daughter Cast in Film of Augusta Drama." *The Augusta Chronicle,* January 20, 1957.

Thigpen, Corbett H., and Hervey M. Cleckley. *The Three Faces of Eve.* New York: McGraw-Hill, 1957.

John Ross, Chief of the Cherokees

Cashin, Edward J. *The Story of Augusta.* Augusta, GA: Richmond County Board of Education, 1980.

Ehle, John. *The Trail of Tears: The Rise and Fall of the Cherokee Nation.* New York: Doubleday, 1989.

Fogleman, Marguerite Flint. *Historical Markers and Monuments of Richmond County, Georgia.* Augusta, GA: Richmond County Historical Society, 1986.

King, Duane, ed. *The Cherokee Indian Nation: A Troubled History.* Knoxville, TN: University of Tennessee Press, 1979.

"More Indian Troubles." *The Augusta Chronicle,* March 2, 1841.

Moulton, Gary E., ed. *The Papers of John Ross, Cherokee Chief.* Athens, GA: University of Georgia Press, 1978.

Taylor-Colbert, Alice. "John Ross (1790–1866)." The New Georgia Encyclopedia. www.georgiaencyclopedia.org.

Preacher's Curse on Jacksonborough

Boyer, Dorothy G. "House Escaped Curse But Not Time." *The Augusta Chronicle,* May 20, 1968.

Boyer, Dorothy G. "Signature of Screven County Notable Has Been Discovered." *The Augusta Chronicle,* February 20, 1970.

Crangle, Susan. "The Curse of Lorenzo Dow." *The Augusta Chronicle, Augusta Herald* (Sunday combined edition), June 7, 1964.

Logue, Frank. "Accept Dow's Challenge." *Tribune & Georgian* (St. Mary's, GA), January 30, 2004.

"Lorenzo Dow." http://en.wikipedia.org/wiki/Lorenzo_Dow.

"Lorenzo Dow." www.1911encyclopedia.org/Lorenzo_Dow.

Palmer, Prentice. "Jacksonboro—Town That Died from a Curse." *The Augusta Chronicle,* July 16, 1969.

Jimmy Carter and the UFO

Associated Press. "Mystery Craft Reported Seen by Plane Pilot." *The Augusta Chronicle,* June 26, 1947.

Floyd, Raymond. "Southern States Looked to Skies in Fall '73." *The Augusta Chronicle,* May 28, 2000.

Floyd, Raymond. "South Has Had Its Share of UFO Sightings." *The Augusta Chronicle,* September 16, 1990.

Hylton, Wil S. "The Gospel According to Jimmy." *GQ,* December 2005.

Report filed by then Georgia Governor Jimmy Carter, International UFO Bureau, Oklahoma City, Oklahoma, September 18, 1973.

Savannah's Waving Girl

Alexander, M. Bishop. "The Waving Girl of Savannah." *The Augusta Chronicle,* December 30, 1923.

Associated Press. "Savannah Lauds Waving Girl." *The Augusta Chronicle,* August 8, 1938.

Associated Press. "Waving Girl Taken by Death in Savannah." *The Augusta Chronicle,* February 9, 1943.

"Sea Girl at Savannah to Get a Loving Cup." *The Augusta Chronicle,* November 5, 1911.

"The Waving Girl Retires from Savannah Harbor." Editorial. *The Augusta Chronicle,* June 19, 1931.

George Washington's Favorite Nephew

Cote, Richard N. *Strength and Honor: The Life of Dolley Madison.* Mt. Pleasant, SC: Corinthian Books, 2005.

Ellis, Joseph J. *His Excellency: George Washington.* New York: Alfred A. Knopf, 2004.

Robertson, Cecelia B. *Respect This Stone, St. Paul's Churchyard, Augusta, Georgia, 1783–1820*. Genealogical research by Robert K. Adams. Augusta, GA: St. Paul's Church, 1976.

Wood, Don C. "Harewood: A Washington Family Legacy." *The Journal* (Martinsburg, WV), March 5, 2009.

The Hollywood Star in Carrollton

Fay, Robin. "Susan Hayward (1917–1975)." The New Georgia Encyclopedia. www.georgiaencyclopedia.org.

Linet, Beverly. *Susan Hayward: Portrait of a Survivor.* New York: Atheneum, 1980.

McClelland, Doug. *Susan Hayward: The Divine Bitch.* New York: Pinnacle Books, 1973.

Schemmel, William. *Georgia Curiosities: Quirky Characters, Roadside Oddities, and Other Offbeat Stuff.* Guilford, CT: Globe Pequot Press, 2003.

Who Built Rock Eagle and the Mounds?

Associated Press. "Mystery Surrounds North Georgia Wall." December 29, 2008. http://chronicle.augusta.com/stories/2008/12/29/met_505775.shtml

Edge, John T. *Georgia.* New York: Compass American Guides (Random House), 2000.

Miles, Jim. *Weird Georgia: Close Encounters, Strange Creatures, and Unexplained Phenomena.* Nashville, TN: Cumberland House, 2000.

Ockershausen, Jane. *The Georgia One-Day Trip Book: A New Way to Explore the State's Romantic Past, Vibrant Present, and Olympian Future.* McLean, VA: EPM Publications, 1993.

Schemmel, William. *Georgia Off the Beaten Path.* Guilford, CT: Globe Pequot Press, 1989.

America's First Wonder Woman

Brehe, S. K., Hugh T. Harrington, and Susan J. Harrington. "Georgia Wonder Phenomenon." The New Georgia Encyclopedia. www.georgiaencyclopedia.org.

Hurst, Lula. *Lula Hurst (The Georgia Wonder) Writes Her Autobiography and for the First Time Explains and Demonstrates the Great Secret of Her Marvelous Power.* Chicago: Psychic Publishing, 1897.

Miles, Jim. *Weird Georgia: Close Encounters, Strange Creatures, and Unexplained Phenomena.* Nashville, TN: Cumberland House, 2000.

Where Is Button Gwinnett?

Deaton, Stan. "Button Gwinnett (1735–1777)." The New Georgia Encyclopedia. www.georgiaencyclopedia.org.

Miller, Zell. *Great Georgians.* Franklin Springs, GA: Advocate Press, 1983.

Perkerson, Medora Field. *White Columns in Georgia.* New York: Holt, Rinehart and Winston, 1952.

Robertson, Cecelia B. *Respect This Stone, St. Paul's Churchyard, Augusta, Georgia, 1783–1820.* Genealogical research by Robert K. Adams. Augusta, GA: St. Paul's Church, 1976.

The Gold and Silver of the Confederacy

"Confederate Gold Guarded to Augusta." *The Augusta Chronicle,* June 8, 1904.

"Dispatch from Our Special Correspondent." The *New York Times,* May 17, 1865.

Georgia Historical Commission. *Georgia Civil War Markers.* Atlanta, GA: Department of Natural Resources, State Parks, Recreation & Historic Sites Division, 1964.

"Penned by Rebel Leaders." The *New York Times,* June 17, 1883.

Perkerson, Medora Field. *White Columns in Georgia.* New York: Holt, Rinehart and Winston, 1952.

Regenstein, Lewis. "My Grandfather and Confederate Gold." Speech to Washington, Georgia, Civil War Roundtable, February 26, 2007. http://lewrockwell.com.

Schemmel, William. *Georgia Curiosities: Quirky Characters, Roadside Oddities, and Other Offbeat Stuff.* Guilford, CT: Globe Pequot Press, 2003.

Schott, Thomas E. *Alexander H. Stephens of Georgia: A Biography.* Baton Rouge, LA: Louisiana State University Press, 1988.

Pasaquan and Other Unusual Places

Associated Press. "Western, Film, Country TV Performer Frankie Scott Dies." April 25, 2004. http://chronicle.augusta.com/stories/042604/met_LG0407-5.shtml

Edge, John T. *Georgia.* New York: Compass American Guides (Random House), 2000.

Historic Thomasville, Georgia: Visitors Guide 2008–2009. Thomasville-Thomas County Visitors Center, 2008.

McCrary, Sarah. "Hot Fun in the Summertime, Classic House." *The Albany Herald,* May 11, 2003.

Schemmel, William. *Georgia Curiosities: Quirky Characters, Roadside Oddities, and Other Offbeat Stuff.* Guilford, CT: Globe Pequot Press, 2003.

Schemmel, William. *Georgia Off the Beaten Path.* Guilford, CT: Globe Pequot Press, 1989.

Scott, Tommy, with Shirley Noe Swiesz and Randall Franks. *Snake Oil, Super Stars, and Me.* Bloomington, IN: AuthorHouse, 2007.

Spector, Tom. *The Guide to the Architecture of Georgia.* Columbia, SC: University of South Carolina Press, 1993.

Circus in the Cemetery

"Columbus, GA, Carnival Train in Head-on Collision." *The Atlanta Constitution,* November 23, 1915.

Culhane, John. *The American Circus: An Illustrated History.* New York: Henry Holt and Company, 1990.

"Head On Collision Has Most Fatal Results." *The Augusta Chronicle,* November 23, 1915.

Murray, Marian. *Circus! From Rome to Ringling.* New York: Appleton-Century-Crofts, 1956.

INDEX

ABOUT THE AUTHOR

 Don Rhodes was born in Gainesville, Texas. He has written for the *Savannah Evening Press, Savannah Morning News, Augusta Chronicle,* and *Augusta Herald.* He is the weekly author of the longest-running country music column in America, "Ramblin' Rhodes," now in its thirty-ninth year. His articles have appeared in such leading national magazines as *Music City News, Country Music, Pickin', Bluegrass Unlimited, Muleskinner News,* and *Bluegrass Now.*

His previous books include *Down Country Roads with Ramblin' Rhodes, Entertainment in Augusta and the CSRA, Ty Cobb: Safe at Home* (Lyons Press), and *Say It Loud! My Memories of James Brown, Soul Brother No. 1* (Lyons Press).

He currently is publications editor of Morris Communications Company and publications manager for the Augusta Futurity and the National Barrel Horse Association.